RICARDO FAYET

How to Market a Book

Overperform in a Crowded Market

Several of the links referenced in the footnotes are affiliate links. All links to Amazon are affiliate links. Other affiliate links are disclosed as such.

First edition

Editing by Rachel Randall
Cover art by Raúl Gil

This book was professionally typeset on Reedsy.
Find out more at reedsy.com

Contents

Introduction

"I need help with marketing" is by far the most frequent message we've received from authors since we started Reedsy in 2014. While the growth of e-books, print on demand, and digital publishing platforms made it easier than ever to publish a (good) book, it also created a publishing landscape where *visibility* quickly became the main struggle for independent authors and traditional publishers alike.

Consistently, more books are published in the current year than in the one before. And while reader surveys seem to indicate that the English-language reader market is still growing, the demand (readers) is undoubtedly growing at a much slower rate than the supply (books).

This negative perspective needs nuance, though. First, the *vast* majority of new books published every year never even sell a few copies. They're published as a hobby, meant for friends and family, and don't receive proper editing, cover design, and of course, marketing.

This still leaves hundreds of thousands of *professional* books to compete for attention and sales on online retailers, in libraries and physical stores, in press articles, on social media and blogs, and so on. And that's where marketing comes in.

Whether you're self-publishing or have a deal with a traditional publisher, the responsibility for marketing your book falls mainly on you. Marketing, just like writing or editing, is a skill, and it is one you cannot afford *not* to learn—that is, if you hope to have any success at selling some copies.

In the past five years at Reedsy, we've helped tens of thousands of authors get their books out there. Many have grown to become full-time authors and make a living off their writing. I have personally consulted and worked hand in hand with hundreds of them, helping them build marketing plans, run online ads, grow their mailing lists, and develop new income streams from their writing.

This book is the result of all these years of teaching and working on marketing with authors across all genres. It compiles all the information you need to get your book in front of readers—and then get those readers to buy it.

It is also the result of a weekly book marketing newsletter I've sent to Reedsy subscribers for the past few years, offering them exclusive information, tips, and trends—many of which I've included in this book. The newsletter has grown hugely in popularity over the years and now has more than 100,000 readers every week. If you're not signed up for it, you can do so here.[1] Of course, these newsletters have all been reworked, updated, and edited to turn this book into more than a simple collection of marketing articles.

Who is this book for?

This book is for anyone who has published or plans to publish a book and wants that book to reach as many readers as possible. That said, the authors who'll find it most useful are those who want to sell more than a few copies and are looking to make a proper living off their writing.

If you're not particularly interested in sales or in building a career as a full-time author, then you won't find much use here. That said, if you picked up this book and committed to reading it, I'm pretty sure you *do* care about sales and readers!

You won't need any previous marketing background to navigate these chapters, because I define each concept in depth and give specific examples. Of course, it's impossible to cover *everything* about book marketing in one book, so in several chapters I point to additional resources where you can learn more about a particular channel.

What will you learn?

There are hundreds of different tactics and strategies you can try to let readers know about your book and get them to buy it. Knowing them all is nice, but it won't do much for you. Instead, you need to find which ones will work for *you*.

So rather than take you through everything you *could* do to market your titles, this book guides you through a step-by-step framework to find the strategies that work *for you and your book*, and start marketing more efficiently.

- Parts I and II focus on this framework, as well as on the mindset you need to adopt to make a living as an author. A lot of this advice isn't purely marketing-related and instead touches on writing craft—but that's because marketing starts well before you even write a book.
- Parts III, IV, and V touch on your book's *appearance* on online retailers (think Amazon, Apple Books, etc.). There's no point in figuring out strategies to bring readers to these retailer pages until they're well-optimized.
- Part VI covers the main marketing element you'll use to connect with your readers: a mailing list.
- Parts VII and VIII dive into the two main marketing channels you can test to get readers to find your book: price promotions and advertising.
- Finally, Part IX looks at additional marketing opportunities beyond the book: box sets, audio, translations, and so on.

Without further ado, let's get started!

I

Mindset and marketing fundamentals

You can try hundreds of different things to market your book. Where most authors fail is not at finding marketing ideas, but at properly testing and implementing them. This first section is all about giving you a proper framework to approach book marketing in a systematic way. And that starts by shifting your perspective from that of the author ... to that of the reader.

1

The mindset

Marketing has become somewhat of a scary word in the world of publishing. The thinking goes that authors are creatives, and as such they're naturally terrible at being salespeople. Almost every day I get an e-mail or request from an author asking if I'd be interested in taking over their marketing, because they just want to focus on writing the next book.

This is the first hurdle many authors have to overcome. Marketing is a different skill, yes. It takes time and dedication, sure. But it's not something you should be afraid of—or at least not for the wrong reasons. Because marketing a book is not about "going out there and finding readers." That is just as spammy and ineffective as it sounds. And it's not how books are sold.

Think about the last book you read: why did you buy it in the first place? Is it because the author somehow tracked you down, cold-called or cold-e-mailed you, or tweeted you saying, "Hey, buy my book!"? Probably not, right? Instead, a friend may have recommended it to you, or you might have come across it while browsing virtual or physical bookshelves.

Here's the thing: *authors don't find readers; readers find books.* That's a simple change in perspective, but a critical one for [RR1] effectively marketing your books. Marketing is not about selling your book to readers. It's about getting readers to find it. Once you shift your perspective to the reader, you start thinking about the number-one question in book marketing: *"How will readers find my book?"*

Now, this is a complicated question with many answers. If you write genre fiction, it's possible that readers will find you through:

- Browsing or searching Amazon, or through an Amazon recommendation e-mail
- A newsletter from one of your author friends recommending your book
- An existing reader sharing your book on Goodreads
- A popular review site
- Etc.

If you write nonfiction, they might find your book through:

- An online search
- An influencer posting about your book
- A podcast
- Your guest post on a major blog
- Etc.

Thinking about where readers find books like yours is the first step toward marketing them. And since I'm confident that you are a reader of the kind of books you write, you should be ideally placed to know where readers tend to find them.

The next step is simple: making sure your books show up in those places. The next few chapters will show you how to achieve that, but in the meantime I want you to take a moment to think about five to ten likely ways readers discover books in your genre. I bet this thought experiment will give you some novel ideas (pun intended) to market your book.

2

The fundamentals

If you start looking for book marketing advice, you'll end up finding heaps of blog posts and videos with titles like "10 things you can try," "50 proven tactics to boost sales," and so on.

These are not necessarily bad posts—heck, we've published one on the Reedsy blog[2] that's full of relevant advice. But the problem is that these posts generally induce writers to try *all of these things at once*, which inevitably leads to the same result: none end up working.

What very few of these posts discuss are the *fundamentals* of marketing a book—and by that I mean the requirements that come with book marketing.

Let's say you're trying to sell a house. You can hire the best realtor, repaint the walls, add stylish décor touches, and offer cookies to potential buyers. But if you have shoddy walls, termites, water damage, or are asking for a price two times the market rate ... no one's going to buy it.

The same goes for your book. If you write a book that readers don't want to read, dress it up with the wrong cover, or price the e-book at fifteen dollars, you'll struggle to sell even one copy, no matter how good your advertising skills are.

There are four marketing fundamentals you simply can't do without, and that's what this chapter is all about. I won't go too in depth into any of them, since most have a dedicated section in this book, but it's important to start by outlining them.

Book marketing fundamental 1: Thou shalt know your target market

Before you even start writing your book, you should make sure you know exactly what *kind* of book you want to write and, more importantly, who will want to read it. The answers to these two questions will inform everything about your marketing strategies.

Take a minute to browse Amazon as a reader. What books are selling best in the genres you're interested in? What do they have in common, not just in content, but in their covers, titles, and book descriptions—and what do they avoid? Is there a niche genre that interests you, that would allow you to gain greater visibility than if you were to compete against the biggest best sellers?

And if you're writing nonfiction, make sure to get a sense of not only the titles you'll be competing with, but also the content they're providing. What are their opinions, and how much detail do they go into? How are the books generally organized—are they workbooks, self-help guides, or in-depth analyses? Write down all your observations so you can refer back to them later.

Once you have a sense of what you'd like to write about, it's time to focus on who reads those genres. Consider the demographics of the target market's average reader: what kind of income level do they have, how quickly do they read books, and what are some of their other common interests?

By doing this, you're starting to construct what's called a "reader avatar"—a stand-in personality that you can refer to when making all your future marketing decisions. Then, whenever you decide to try something new, consider the best way to reach that person. After all, the best marketing strategy is specific; trying to market to *everyone* will mean that you'll reach *no one*.

Book marketing fundamental 2: Thou shalt have the right product for your target

Now that you know what your target readers look like, you'll need to deliver a quality product that matches—or, better yet, exceeds—their expectations. And when it comes to marketing a book, the first step is, of course, writing a book that speaks to your audience.

Remember that market research you just did? It's time to put it to work. Every genre and category, whether fiction or nonfiction, has its own rules about what sells best and what readers prefer. Look back at your research notes and ask yourself if you've matched the best sellers in your field when it comes to:

- Tone and overall style
- Structure and story arcs
- Character types
- Popular tropes
- Type and density of information

If anything is lacking, now's the time to shore it up! And if you're ever unsure whether your work's on target, don't worry—this is what Part II of this book is all about.

Book marketing fundamental 3: Thou shalt learn the secrets of Amazon

Amazon is a kingpin in the publishing world. Even if you decide to "sell wide" and build your presence across multiple retailers, you'll still be making most of your sales through Amazon. So you really can't afford to ignore how it works, and specifically how readers find books on Amazon.

Learn how to leverage its algorithms and climb the ranks to the right level of visibility, and Amazon will even take over part of your marketing efforts for you (for free!) by automatically suggesting your books to readers in your genre.

Sound too good to be true? It's not, and you'll discover why in Parts III and IV. And since Amazon is not the *only* retailer out there, you'll also find an in-depth analysis of Apple Books, Google Play, and Kobo in Part V.

Book marketing fundamental 4: Thou shalt establish your web presence

1. An author website

If readers really enjoy your book, they'll want to find out more about you. If they google your name, your website better show up at the top of the search results. How you build your website depends entirely on what you want readers to do once they've found it. Do you want them to sign up for your newsletter? Place that sign-up link front and center, add an incentive, and even install exit pop-ups. Do you want them to buy your other books? Make sure the covers are clearly visible, with buttons to buy them on every bookstore where they're available.

If you don't have a website already, I have a simple recommendation: hire a professional website developer with previous experience building websites *for authors.* You'll find a bunch of them on Reedsy, all vetted by our team, who'll be able to deliver a perfect website.

"What's an alternative for those of us who don't have the budget for that?" Well, you can learn how to do it yourself. But trust me, the time you'll spend on this task will make you regret your decision. More importantly, it's time better spent building ...

2. A mailing list

I truly cannot stress enough the importance of a mailing list. A mailing list is the number-one way to grow and reach your fan base—yes, even in today's social-media-saturated world—and neglecting to learn how to use it effectively will only lose you sales. Be sure to set up and nurture your list right from the start. And if you're ever unsure how best to go about that, don't worry; Part VI of this book covers mailing lists in depth.

Speaking of social media, while these platforms can be incredibly powerful for many authors, I don't consider them a must-have. You can sell a lot of books even if you're not active on Twitter, Facebook, Instagram, and so on.

And while you could technically build your fan base on a social medium (e.g., a Facebook group) rather than through your mailing list, you don't *control* social media. Sites and apps can change the rules without notice and cut you off from your audience, as Facebook did a few years ago by limiting the reach of Pages. That won't happen with a mailing list where *you* set the rules.

These are the four fundamentals you should *always* keep in mind before you do any other marketing. You'll notice that none of them will magically bring readers to discover your books. For that, you'll need to use marketing tactics—or channels—like advertising or price promotions.

3

The channels

One of the first (and only) books I read about startup marketing, with a view to apply its advice to growing Reedsy, was *Traction: How Any Startup Can Achieve Explosive Customer Growth*.[3]

Published in 2014, it's a fairly old book now, and I wouldn't necessarily recommend it anymore to startup founders. However, one of its central marketing principles remains crucial to *anyone* trying to market *anything*—and yes, that includes you and your book. In fact, I interviewed one of the authors of *Traction* a few years ago, who said as much.[4]

See, the core idea of the book is that there are hundreds of different ways, or "channels," to market a product or grow a company. The secret of success is not to do all of them, or even as many as possible. Instead, it's to find the *one or two channels that work* for your company and focus all your energy and resources on *just those*.

I find that this concept translates particularly well to book marketing. In the book realm, these "channels" include Facebook ads, Amazon ads, Book-Bub ads, price promotions, e-mail marketing, group promos, newsletter swaps, Amazon SEO, Goodreads promos, guest posting, events, social media, and more.

When you're starting out, you'll probably be tempted to do all those things, because you've read about them everywhere. But that presents the same problem as trying to be on all the social media platforms: first, you don't have the time for that, and second, you probably won't be *good* at all of those platforms.

Finding the sweet spot

Take me, for example. I love helping authors market their books, and I've run Facebook, Amazon, and BookBub ads; built mailing lists; used reader magnets; organized price promotions; and done everything else under the sun.

So I've *done* all those things, but I know I'm a lot better at some of them than others. When it comes to advertising, for instance, I know I'm much stronger working with Facebook ads than with Amazon ads or BookBub ads.

Other authors, like David Gaughran, are pros at BookBub ads, but hate Amazon ads. And still others have cracked Amazon ads, but don't even touch the other two platforms.

We all have different sensibilities to different marketing channels—that's just how we are.

But how *we* are is just one part of the equation. The other part is how *our readers* are. You might be a pro at BookBub ads, but if your book is on a niche nonfiction topic, BookBub's audience for that topic will be pretty limited—and running ads there won't be effective for long.

While some channels will work for almost any genre (e.g., Amazon ads), many others will only be suited to some genres (or even some particular books).

So how do you find that sweet spot? How do you find a channel you're good at *and* that resonates with your readers?

Well, you test. But the thing is …

You can't test everything at once

The other core principle of *Traction* intersects with one of the main mistakes I see authors making when it's time to market their books: they're trying way too many things *at the same time*.

11

It's natural, after all: if you don't know what's going to work, you might as well try ten different things at once to find the one or two that *will* work.

But the problem is that you'll never manage to get a channel to work if you're not focusing all of your energy on it.

Let's look at an example. You just published your book, but it's not selling after one week. So you panic (naturally) and perhaps start googling "book marketing ideas." That's when you find all of these things you "should be doing" but aren't. So you could:

· Change your Amazon keywords
· Start a mailing list
· Start boosting your posts on Facebook
· Start an Amazon ads campaign with a few obvious keywords
· Book a bunch of price promotion sites
· Create a "reader group" on Facebook
· Start tweeting five times a day
· Reach out to fifty book bloggers in your genre
· Etc.

And you know what? None of these channels is going to work, because you're going to execute all of them badly. Even if you execute one well and see your book's sales increase, you won't know which channel was responsible for it!

All the channels I've listed above take *time* to learn and master. Until you've put in that time, you won't be able to test them properly.

So whenever you're feeling overwhelmed by marketing (or whenever your to-do list gets out of hand), take a breather and reevaluate: "Do I really need to do all of this?"

Pick only two things, and spend a month focusing on them. Take courses (you'll find tons of free ones on Reedsy Learning), ask colleagues, read blog posts, and then put in the time to properly test each channel.

That's the only way you'll find that sweet spot—or, in other words, that golden channel that will change your marketing forever.

4

The silent majority

Back in 2020, just before the COVID-19 situation exploded, I attended the first "Self Publishing Show Live" event put together by the Self Publishing Formula team in London. A lot of great authors attended and presented, but the talk that impacted me the most was given by thriller writer L. J. Ross, arguably one of the UK's most successful indie authors of all time.

She started self-publishing early on, back when there was less competition (and different rules). But that was also a time when resources like Reedsy or Self Publishing Formula didn't exist, meaning that indie authors were very much left on their own to figure things out.

During her talk she shared one piece of advice about the importance of the "silent majority" that really resonated with me. In her words, more or less: "As an author, you tend to always hear from the outliers: those who really love or hate your book. But what you want is for the silent majority to spread word of mouth."

Let's think about this in terms of reviews. Out of one hundred readers who buy and read your book, how many will leave a review? At best, five or ten. And the truth is no matter how glowing or critical the opinions in those reviews are, they're going to be less important than the opinion of the silent majority: all the readers who *won't* e-mail you or leave a review.

If sixty out of these ninety silent readers enjoyed your book enough to recommend it to two to three friends each, your book will automatically sell another 120 to 180 copies—without you having to lift a finger.

And if 60 percent of these new readers each tell two friends about your book, that's even more copies sold. And if ... well, you get the gist. In a nutshell, the same logic that applies to the coronavirus applies to word of mouth: it makes a book go viral.

But here's the problem with word of mouth: you can't control it, and you have no way of forecasting it. This is because the readers who'll spread it the most are the *silent majority*: they won't tell *you* how much they enjoyed the book—they'll only tell their friends.

Giving the initial push

"Great, so you're telling me about a marketing thing I can't control?"

Yes and no. There *are* things you can do to encourage word of mouth. The first is obvious: write a great book.

That's easier said than done, of course, and it can mean many things depending on who your target audience is. But essentially you need to write a book that will grab the average reader (in other words, the silent majority) so much that they won't be able to shut up about it for a week. We've all read books like that. We know the feeling. That's what you should try to elicit in the reader. Or in the words of another self-publishing pioneer, J. A. Konrath, "Don't write shit."

"So I just have to write a really, really amazing book and I won't have to market it?"

Unfortunately, no. Certainly not anymore. Even if your book is worthy of word of mouth, you still have to find the first one hundred readers (and usually many more) to start carrying it in the first place.

Karen Inglis, an international bestselling children's book author and another panelist at the conference, shared a great illustration of this concept. Her main book only took off when she started running Amazon ads to advertise it. But she found out that the ads she ran, though they gave her a positive return on investment, were responsible for only *25 percent* of the sales she started generating.

In other words, for every reader who purchased a book as a result of her ads, three more ended up buying it through ... you guessed it, word of mouth.

So that's all you need: a really, really, really great book and a little push to get the ball rolling. Again, easier said than done, especially considering that both factors in this equation (the great book and the push) each require getting a huge number of subfactors right.

But overall, this is a good framework you can use to divide your marketing efforts:

- On one hand, efforts focused on making the book(s) as sellable and recommendable as possible
- On the other hand, efforts focused on giving the book(s) the initial push they'll need to start selling

Because that push will get you nowhere unless you've got a perfect product, the next two parts in this book will focus on the first bit: *creating a sellable and recommendable book (or series of books).*

II

Writing to market

Marketing doesn't start when your book is finished. It starts before you even outline it. The first step toward creating a best-selling book is knowing exactly for whom the book is intended—in other words, knowing your market and writing to market.

Now, that's a controversial opinion: you might think that art should never be restrained by marketing considerations. And that's fine, as long as you don't care about selling such art. If you do, keep reading.

5

Finding Your Niche

One thing I quickly figured out while attending conferences and meeting successful indie authors is that a vast majority of them share a similar approach to writing and publishing.

At the end of the day, we can talk all we want about advertising, mailing lists, price promotions, and reviews ... but if you don't have the right product and mindset, you'll have little chance of making a living as a self-publishing author.

So what do all successful indie authors have in common?

1. They have found their place in the market (i.e., a profitable niche to write in).
2. They know the niche well enough to write in it and build a sizablecatalog of books in that market (i.e., they know how to write and publish *fast*).
3. They build bridges, or arcs, between their books and organize them in series or universes.

These three key aspects are the focus of the next few chapters.

Write what you know, or write to market?

If there's one thing writers love to do, it's give advice to other writers. From "Show, don't tell" to "Kill your darlings," countless (often misattributed) quotes from famous authors have become popular enough to turn into writing *rules* every author should abide by.

That said, when it comes to picking a book topic, you may come across two often conflicting yet equally popular "rules": "Write what you know" vs. "Write to market."

The first one, "Write what you know," is self-explanatory: the more familiar you are with your topic or genre of choice, the more you can anchor your writing on things you *know*—whether that's your own experiences or expertise (nonfiction) or genre tropes you can memorize by heart (fiction). The wider your knowledge on the chosen topic or genre, the easier the process and the stronger your writing.

The second one, "Write to market," focuses less on the writing process, or even on quality. It's more concerned with the business side of things: you should write something you know will fit perfectly into an existing market.

So which one do *I* think you should go for? Well, it depends on your goal. If you want to finally finish that first book, then you should definitely write what you know. If your aim is to *sell* that book and you like the idea of ultimately living off your writing, then you should write to market.

Finding your niche

Of course, that's easier said than done. First, you need to find a market, or niche, to write in. There are several ways to go about that, but the most effective one is to turn to the biggest book retailer: Amazon.

Analyzing Amazon categories

When it comes to identifying rising trends and niches in the book industry, no one has more data than Amazon. They constantly reshuffle the Browse categories in their Kindle Store based on that data. Keeping a close eye on emerging categories can be an extremely effective way to spot growing niches before they become saturated.

But how do you know whether a niche category is big or not? Well, you can trust your hunches. Or you can use a proper scientific method to analyze what little data Amazon makes available.

First, go to the Kindle Store best sellers page; you can find it by googling "Kindle e-book best sellers." You'll see a list of genres in the left sidebar—what we call the "Browse" categories—and you can click on any of them to access subcategories. Have a poke around, and select a few categories you might be interested in.

Next, open the pages of the first five books in each of these categories and scroll down to the "Product Details" section. There, you'll see the book's rank within the Kindle or Books store. This rank is a reflection of how well the book sells—and therefore, the ranks of the top five books in a given category are a reflection of how competitive the category is.

For example, if you find that the top five books in category A all have ranks below one thousand on Amazon, while only the first book in category B has a rank below that number, you'll immediately know that category A is much bigger (and more competitive) than category B.

To further the analysis, several rank-to-sales calculators out there allow you to view the estimated daily sales of a book based on its Amazon rank. My favorite is the one from Kindlepreneur.[5] By using it, you can find out, more or less, how many copies the top books in any category are selling. If the books are selling well, it means there are a lot of readers in that category and you've probably identified a market worth writing in.

Publisher Rocket

If you're a heavy Amazon ads advertiser, or if you're looking to ramp up your Amazon keyword and category analysis game, then I recommend you purchase Publisher Rocket.[6] It's an app designed by Dave Chesson that automates the process I describe above. For example, if you were interested in entering the cozy mystery market, you'd type "cozy" into Publisher Rocket's "Categories" tool, and you'd get this:

Category Search		Both	Book	eBook	Q cozy		
CATEGORY	ABSR of #1	SALES to #1	ABSR of #10	SALES to #10	CATEGORY PAGE		
Books > Mystery, Thriller & Suspense > Mystery > Cozy	111	289	129	271	Check it out		
Books > Mystery, Thriller & Suspense > Mystery > Cozy > Animals	287	165	1777	72	Check it out		
Books > Mystery, Thriller & Suspense > Mystery > Cozy > Crafts & Hobbies	287	165	3129	29	Check it out		
Books > Mystery, Thriller & Suspense > Mystery > Cozy > Culinary	756	83	2731	39	Check it out		
Kindle Store > Kindle eBooks > Mystery, Thriller & Suspense > Mystery > Cozy	108	955	730	124	Check it out		
Kindle Store > Kindle eBooks > Mystery, Thriller & Suspense > Mystery > Cozy > Animals	294	343	2272	85	Check it out		
Kindle Store > Kindle eBooks > Mystery, Thriller & Suspense > Mystery > Cozy > Crafts & Hobbies	294	343	2870	73	Check it out		
Kindle Store > Kindle eBooks > Mystery, Thriller & Suspense > Mystery > Cozy > Culinary	819	118	2650	77	Check it out		

This tells me that the "Cozy > Animals" category on the Kindle Store is pretty big: the first book in that category sells an average 343 copies a day, and the tenth book sells eighty-five copies a day. Not bad, right?

K-lytics reports

If you're a proper data nerd, or if you're serious about *writing to market*, then you're probably a good candidate for K-lytics,[7] the most advanced Kindle Store analytics tool available to indie authors. Just a word of warning: it's pricey, as their plans start at thirty-seven dollars per month. (In comparison, Publisher Rocket is a one-time ninety-seven-dollar purchase.)

The great thing about K-lytics is that they release monthly reports that zero in on specific markets and analyze all the niches in each of these markets. If there's a rising trend somewhere on Amazon, they'll spot it for you.

Of course, finding that niche is only the first step. In many regards, it's the easiest, because the next one is actually writing the book(s). And because you're *writing to market* rather than *writing what you know*, you'll need to do a lot of research on that genre (i.e., a lot of reading) before you know enough to write in it.

6

Entering your niche

Once you've settled on the niche you want to write in, the next step is to make preparations to launch your first books in that niche. And yes, I use the plural deliberately here, but we'll get to that in a moment. In the meantime, what you really need to do before you start writing the first book is research.

Research your niche

I know, I know—this book is supposed to focus on marketing. But the thing is that the product is one of the central elements of any marketing effort. And the success of any product is contingent on the existence of a "product-market fit."

In other words, once you've found a profitable (and ideally growing) niche, you need to write books that readers in your niche will love. And so it follows that your first step is to thoroughly research this niche.

Read the best-selling books in your market

This may seem like obvious advice, but there's no better way to get to know a genre than to read a bunch of successful books in that genre. That said, you shouldn't just read them for pleasure, as an average reader would. You should read them with an analytical mind, asking questions.

For fiction, ask:

- What are the commonalities among these different books?
- What story structure do they typically follow?
- What conflicts do the characters face, and what are the stakes?
- What point(s) of view is the author using?

For nonfiction, ask:

- How is the book structured?
- Is the information conveyed through storytelling or in a more academic way?
- What is the tone of the book (inspirational, humoristic, etc.)?

The goal of all these questions is to help you identify the *tropes* of your genre—which is the first step toward incorporating them into your books.

Seek genre-specific writing advice

If you're a fiction writer looking to break into a new genre, reading books in that genre might not be sufficient to learn how to *write* in that genre. In that case, seeking writing advice can be a good idea.

For example, if you're looking to break into the paranormal romance (PNR) market and you've never written a sex scene or a love triangle with shapeshifters before, you might want to read a book or a few blog posts specifically about that. If you're looking to write epic Arthurian fantasy for the first time, reading about worldbuilding techniques won't hurt, either. And if you want to enter the cozy mystery market, then you probably want to do some reading on how to place clever clues in your story.

Make some friends along the way

All this might sound like a lot of work when you're just *researching*. But this phase can amount to a lot more than research.

If in addition to reading the best-selling books in this new niche you also review the books, join authors' mailing lists and reader groups, and even reach out to authors, you may end up building relationships with the heavy hitters in your target genre. This can be instrumental for when you finally prepare to launch *your* books.

That said, don't be that sleazy author who's just looking to get some free writing advice or piggyback on someone else's audience. Be a nice person and build a genuine relationship without asking for any favors. In other words, make some friends.

Build your catalog

There's always a sort of gold-rush phase when a new niche starts becoming widely popular and attracting "neighboring genre" authors. It happened in 2018–19 with the literary role-playing game (LitRPG) genre: countless fantasy and sci-fi authors released new series aimed at breaking into this new, burgeoning market.

If you've identified a niche that looks promising, chances are you're not the only one. In many ways, that's a good thing—it allows you to build relationships with existing authors in that genre. But it also means you can't just publish one book and expect it to pay for your early retirement on a tropical island.

If you're serious about breaking into a new genre, you'll need more than one book. Ideally, you should plan for a series and be ready to rapid-release the first few books.

Rapid-release

Rapid-releasing is a term that started to appear in 2017–18 to describe a marketing technique growing in popularity to launch a new series. Instead of writing and releasing book one, then writing and releasing book two, etc., some authors wrote the first three or more books in a series and then rapid-released them over a short period of time (generally, every thirty days).

What is the purpose of rapid-releasing titles? It's a way to leverage the visibility online retailers (mostly Amazon) give to new releases. We'll delve more into rapid-releasing in the Amazon Marketing section of this book, but for now, the key takeaway is that new books on Amazon get extra visibility for a period of thirty days after launch. So what happens when you rapid-release three books thirty days apart? You benefit from that extra visibility for three straight months, which tends to make an enormous difference. There are other benefits as well: for example, readers don't have to wait for months to get the next book—a time during which they could easily forget about you.

Of course, this strategy requires you to bank on the success of these first three books and have the patience and discipline to get all of them ready before the rapid release. It also requires you to keep up a steady publishing cadence afterwards—you can't release the first three titles thirty days apart and then release only one book a year. This would make readers angry, and angry readers make for negative reviews.

"So I need to be able to write several books every year?" you might be wondering. In a word, yes. I'd say 90 percent of the successful indie authors I know write at least two books a year. The most successful ones probably publish more than three or four.

Of course, that leaves 10 percent who do manage to make a living from one book a year (or less). I'm definitely *not* saying it's impossible. It requires a different mindset, and more savviness when it comes to marketing, but it's doable. Jami Albright, a successful romance author, is a perfect example. (You can listen to our Reedsy Bestseller podcast episode with her to hear more.[8]) But it's true that one of the best things you can do for your writing career is to work on increasing your output. If you're able to put out two, three, or more (good) books a year, you'll have a much easier time entering and establishing yourself in new niches.

7

Series and universes

Once you've published a few books in a niche, the next step is to *stay in that niche*. This is something most of us creatives will find incredibly difficult. Do you know that feeling when you're working on book two in a series and an idea suddenly pops into your head for a completely different book in a completely different genre—and suddenly you just *have* to write that one rather than keep working on your series?

Well, creativity is both a blessing and a curse, because from a marketing standpoint, the example above is akin to throwing all your existing assets out the window and starting from scratch. Sometimes, that can be necessary (e.g., if you got your niche wrong in the first place). But most of the time, it's a waste of all the work you've put in so far.

As I mentioned in the last chapter, publishing one book—even if it's in the fastest-growing, least-competitive niche—is rarely enough to pay the bills. If you're planning on becoming a full-time author, you will most likely need to publish *several* books in a niche. If you write one here, one there, and another one elsewhere again, you'll have to market each of these three books to entirely different audiences. That's as inefficient as it gets, marketing-wise.

Instead, if you manage to hook a reader into a series, they will likely buy *all the books* in that series.

The power of series

Let's say you're able to sell a standalone book to one thousand readers. Depending on its price, that book might make you $350 (book priced at $0.99, with 35 percent in royalties) to $4,200 (book priced at $5.99 with 70 percent in royalties). But what if that book actually wasn't a standalone, but book one in a series of five (all priced at $2.99), and those one thousand readers read all of them? You'd make:

```
$2.99 × 5 × $0.70 × 1,000 = $10,465
```

And if you had ten books in that series? You'd make about $21,000.

In the end, it's just as hard to *sell* a standalone as it is to sell book one of a series. It'll take the same marketing effort (e.g., the same amount of advertising money). But in the case of the series, the potential returns are much greater.

"And what about us nonfiction authors?" I can hear you saying. Well, this applies just as well to most nonfiction. Are you familiar with Tim Ferriss's 4-Hour books? Or with the multiauthored Miracle Morning books? Or with the Chicken Soup for the Soul collections? Well, guess what? All of these are effectively nonfiction *series* in specific niches: productivity, wellness, and inspiration, respectively.

If you're an expert on a specific topic and you want to make money from writing about it, the easiest way to achieve that is by writing *several* books, giving them proper branding, and linking them into a series.

See, most retailers (Amazon, Apple, Google Play, Kobo, etc.) have what we call "series pages." These are used to showcase all of the books in a given series, not only on the series page, but on each book's product page.

The Miracle Morning (14 book series)

Kindle Edition

From Book 1: "Hal Elrod is a genius and his book *The Miracle Morning* has been magical in my life. What Hal has done is taken the best practices, developed over centuries of human consciousness development, and condensed the 'best of the best' into a daily morning ritual. A ritual that is now part of my day."

—**Robert Kiyosaki, bestselling author of *Rich Dad Poor Dad***

| All Formats | Kindle Edition |

What's being widely regarded as "one of the most life changing books ever written" may be the simplest approach to achieving everything you've ever

∨ Read more

☐ Hide books already in your library

1

The Miracle Morning: The Not-So-Obvious Secret Guaranteed to Transform Your Life (Before 8AM)
by Hal Elrod (Author) , Robert Kiyosaki (Foreword)
☆☆☆☆☆ (4,259)
Currently Unavailable
"Hal Elrod is a genius and his book *The Miracle Morning* has been magical in my life. What Hal has done is taken the best practices, developed over centuries of human consciousness development, and condensed the 'best of

∨ Read more
Other Formats: Audible Audiobook , Hardcover , Paperback

2

The Miracle Morning for Real Estate Agents: It's Your Time to Rise and Shine

The series collection page for the Miracle Morning books

31

The series carousel on the first Miracle Morning book's product page

This instantly lets the reader know that you have *a lot* of material ready for them. In nonfiction, it instantly increases your perceived authority in the eyes of the reader. (*"Wow, this author hasn't just written* one *book about growing orchids, but a whole series!"*)

In fiction, most commercial genres are heavily dominated by series. This is because fiction readers generally get the most attached to *characters*. Do you know that feeling when you finish a book and you just *need* to know what happens next to a particular character? That's why series are so popular—they allow readers to stick with the characters they love.

From series to ... universes

Alright, let's say you've found that awesome niche you want to write in. You've rapid-released the first three books, then published three to four books a year in that series, and finally ended with a ninth and final book. What's next?

You can only carry a series for so long. For a fiction series, you need to close your story and character arcs at some point; otherwise you're just dragging out the narrative for the sake of it. Think about a longtime favorite television series in which nothing interesting has happened in the last few seasons. That's what I'm talking about. You don't want to be that author.

But at the same time, it *is* a shame to stop capitalizing on the success of an existing series. You don't want to lose these hard-earned reader fans by starting a completely unrelated series that they won't want to get into.

So what's the answer? Universes. Most people think of universes as worlds or franchises. The Wizarding World is a universe, for example. Star Wars is another one.

I like to think of universes as series of series (how meta, right?). The Wizarding World, for example, has two series in it (for now): Harry Potter and Fantastic Beasts. And just like a series creates bridges between each book, a universe creates bridges between each series. And readers use these bridges to make their way from one book to another, and from one series to another.

Suddenly, those one thousand readers who read book one don't just read the other nine books in your series; they also read the ten books in the three other series in your universe. Congratulations—you've just quadrupled your revenue from that first series. To go back to our example, you went from $21,000 to $84,000.

But it doesn't stop there, because these other series will also attract *their own readers*. And these readers will also read all your other books in all your other series in that universe.

So you go from one series that earns $21,000 to four series that earn $84,000 *each*. That's $336,000 total. And that's just from four thousand readers! (Granted, they're ultra-fan readers.)

I know, I know. These calculations are overly simplistic. Not everyone reading book one of series one will read book two, let alone all the other books in all the other series. But you get the point: building bridges between each book in a series allows you to *multiply their revenue potential*.

Math and money aside, universes are also a great way of rewarding your readers and building a loyal fan base. You can include Easter eggs in each series that only readers of the other series will get. You can feature the same character or place across different series. You can also create novellas or short stories that *bridge* your series together. A great example of this is Brandon Sanderson's Cosmere universe. Most of his series take place in different worlds, have different magic systems and different characters, etc., but they are all a part of the same Cosmere universe—which only becomes clear to readers once they read several series, creating an "aha!" moment that makes them feel special. (I know it worked for me.)

The craft of writing in universes

Writing series and universes that pull readers in and keep them reading is much easier said than done. It takes careful plotting, as each book must have a story arc that fits within a bigger series arc. The same goes for characters: they must evolve in each book, but have enough space to grow and change in future books. You can't end all your books with cliffhangers (unless you're George R. R. Martin), but you also can't end them perfectly resolved; otherwise readers won't be enticed to buy the next one.

Instead you can use something I'm stealing from a great talk Michael Anderle gave at 20Books Vegas 2018:[9] the concept of "open loops." These are basically mini cliffhangers, unresolved conflicts unrelated to the main plot, but instead connected to the characters or smaller subplots.

For example, your main plot may be about a secret agent trying to escape terrorists in a foreign country—but that agent also starts a romance with a local person. When you resolve the main plot (the agent manages to get back home in one piece), you can leave an open loop about their relationship and whether the terrorists might use one to get to the other.

That's just one way of doing it, though. You may prefer straight cliffhangers, or you may have captivating enough characters that readers will jump to the next book even if all conflicts are seemingly resolved. All in all, you need to find what works best for your genre and your series. For that, go back to my initial advice: read and analyze the best-selling series in your genre, and in particular how they manage to pull readers through.

Marketing universes

The great thing about universes is that they simplify your marketing strategy *a lot*. When you have all your books in series and universes, you don't need to advertise and push every book you release; you need only to heavily and constantly market book one in each series.

These first books are the gates into your universe. If you manage to get readers to enter through one of the gates, there's a *probability* they'll cross all the bridges, read all your books, and never leave your universe!

This *probability* is what you'll often hear referred to as "read through." And that's what the next chapter in this series (hehe) is all about.

8

Read through

I have to warn you: this chapter contains some math. It's not scary math, though, and it's absolutely key to understand if you're going to market a series of books, because it all revolves around *read through*.

Read through (RT) is the percentage of readers of a given book in your series who go on to read the next book.

For example, if one hundred people read your first book and seventy-five of them go on to buy and read your second one, your read through from book one to book two is 75 percent. Then, if sixty of these seventy-five end up reading book three, your read through from book one to book three is 60 percent.

The read through metric is crucial to any series writer for many reasons—mostly related to advertising and calculating ROI. But before we get to that, it's important to understand what RT actually represents.

Nonmathematical implications of read through

At its core, read through is the best scientific measure of how "unputdownable" your series is. If 80 percent of readers who buy book one go on to read your entire series, then you've created something that turns four out of five casual readers into hardcore fans. Well done!

On the other hand, if only 25 percent of readers who buy book one end up buying book two, then you know you have a problem with book one or how you're marketing it. Maybe your story (or your argument, for nonfiction) isn't compelling enough and readers don't even finish the book. Or perhaps you're targeting it at the wrong people with unsuitable Amazon categories or keywords, or with a book cover that gives the wrong impression. Or maybe book two is priced too high.

In those cases, it's hard to know exactly *what* is wrong. But you can sometimes find out by reading your reviews (if all your write-ups mention "bad editing," you know what to fix first ...) or by testing a specific factor (drop the price of book two and see what happens).

You should regularly monitor read through across your whole series (and not just from book one to book two), as that will tell you *where* you start losing the most readers. For example, if RT from book one to book four is 60 percent, but only 25 percent from book one to book five, then you know you're losing a ton of readers at book four! Again, there can be hundreds of different reasons for that, and RT alone won't tell you which one it is or how to fix it. But at least you'll know there's a problem.

"OK, you've convinced me to look at your read through thing. But where do I find that info?" Well, you (or rather my rhetoric impersonation of you) just asked the million-dollar question.

Monitoring read through

Amazon and other e-retailers give you very little information about what your readers do. They tell you how many sales you made on your books in a given time period ... and that's about it.

So how do you figure out what percentage of readers make it from one book to another? Well, the only way to do that—for now—is to estimate it.

To do so, you can look at your sales report (I highly recommend using Book Report[10] for Amazon) and check the sales of both books.

To get the RT estimate of any book, just divide its sales number by that of book one in the series. For example, if you have the following sales report:

```
Book one: 500 sales
Book two: 350 sales
Book three: 340 sales
Book four: 300 sales
Book five: 200 sales
```

Then your read through estimations would be:

```
RT2: 350 ÷ 500 = 70 percent
RT3: 340 ÷ 500 = 68 percent
RT4: 300 ÷ 500 = 60 percent
RT5: 200 ÷ 500 = 40 percent
```

Now, this method comes with a lot of flaws, the main one being that sales numbers can easily be influenced by *external factors* that have nothing to do with the natural readthrough progression. For example:

- You just launched the latest book in the series.
- You ran a price promotion or free promotion on one of your sequels.
- You got special visibility from Amazon (e.g., Daily Deal) on one of your sequels.

In each of these cases, the book in question would have an artificially inflated number of sales—sometimes even more than book one. So if you were to look at the last ninety days of sales for your series and calculate RT using the formula above, you'd get a percentage well over 100 percent, which would make no sense.

"So how do you avoid these external factors (as much as possible)?" Well, you pick a time period for the sales report that is long enough to be statistically significant (I recommend *at least* ninety days), during which none of your books (except book one) received any kind of special promo or attention.

Alternatively, you can look at your *all-time* sales numbers, as the statistical pollution of promos should be dwarfed by regular sales in that overall time period.

A silver lining?

The sales data method for estimating read through is simple enough, and by selecting the right time period you can get relatively "clean" data. However, it's still far from ideal.

What would be ideal (or "normal," depending on your point of view) would be for retailers to actually *tell you* what your read through is. Something like:

```
"In the past [number of months], [XX percent] of readers who
bought book one in your series actually read it. Of the readers
who read it:
- XX% went on to purchase book 2;
- XX% also purchased book 3;
- XX% purchased book 4;
- etc."
```

Retailers *have this data.* They're just not sharing it with you. Now, the good news is that some of them might start doing it very soon. Two big (non-Amazon) retailers mentioned to me back in 2019 that they were planning to release such data to their authors in the near future (one for free, the other for a fee).

When that happens, you'll be able to use that data in your ROI calculations, making them all the more accurate. In the meantime, if you sell enough books on a wide retailer, you can try asking for your read through data. Some of them have been sharing it privately with their high-earning authors—so it's worth a shot. One caveat, of course, is that read through might vary from one retailer to another. So what you get on Kobo, Apple, or Barnes & Noble might be very different from what you get on Amazon. But if we're holding our breath for Amazon to release their data ... well, we can hold it for a *looooong* time.

That's all you need to know about calculating and analyzing read through! I wanted to discuss read through early on because I genuinely believe it's the most important data for series writers to monitor—and by now you should know that if you want to make a living writing, you should be a series writer.

You'll find another chapter about read through in Part VIII of this book, focused more on its mathematical implications when running ads to promote your books. But before we get to ads—or any marketing channel you can use to drive *traffic* to your book pages—it's important to first talk about *conversion*.

III

Conversion

Now that you know the best formula for making a living from your writing, it's time to focus on how to market these entry points into your series and universes. Often authors will confuse "marketing my books" with "driving eyeballs to my books," but that's skipping an ever-important first step: optimizing your product and packaging to make sure any eyeballs that see it want to buy it.

9

The conversion funnel

In the very first chapter, I explained how *finding readers* is about making sure readers *find you*. Or rather, find your book. But that's only part of the equation.

Once a reader lands on your book's Amazon page or picks it up from the shelf in a physical bookstore, there's still a chance—a high chance, actually—that they'll put it back or leave.

I've been running ads for several authors for several years now, and the highest conversion rates I've seen on Amazon book pages (for *paid* books) have been around 30 to 35 percent. This means that for every three readers who visit your book page, two will leave without buying. And this is for *exceptional cases*. The conversion rate for most books is more in the 0 to 10 percent range.

So what do you need to sell books? Well, you need people to find your book (traffic), and then you need these people to *buy it* (conversion). Which leads us to the famous e-commerce formula:

```
Traffic × Conversion = Sales
```

Most authors, when thinking about book marketing, think *only* about traffic. So my goal in this chapter is to get you thinking about conversion.

What the heck is a conversion funnel?

You've probably heard the term *funnel* before, but what does it mean, exactly? In a nutshell, a funnel encapsulates the steps a consumer has to take before making a purchase.

You attract lots of consumers with a wide-reaching campaign, akin to the wide brim at the top of a funnel, but the number who will buy your product is more like the smaller tapered part at the bottom. Your goal is to coax the ones at the top to the bottom over time.

For instance, a car dealership's funnel for a customer named Henry could look something like this:

```
Henry views a TV ad about a new car. > Henry goes to the
dealership to check out the new car. > Henry does a test drive.
> Henry buys the car.
```

Now, at every point in the funnel, the dealership might *lose* potential customers for a variety of reasons, including:

- They might view the ad, but not like it.
- They might go to the dealership, but be disappointed by the look of the car.
- They might find the car horrible to drive.

So what does the funnel look like for a reader who finds your book online?

```
Henry comes across your book on Amazon. > Henry looks at the
cover and title. > Henry clicks on it. > Henry reads your blurb.
> Henry checks out your reviews. > Henry opens the preview to
read the first few pages. > Henry buys the e-book or paperback.
```

Not every reader will be like Henry and go through *all* these steps. But many will, so the easiest way to increase your sales *right now* is to thoroughly audit all these steps and try to identify where you're losing potential readers.

Conversion matters more than traffic

While traffic and conversion are both important, when it comes to getting sales, I believe conversion is not only overlooked by authors, it's *more important* than traffic. A simple change in your blurb might get your Amazon book page to convert at 15 percent instead of 5 percent. And this will effectively (and instantly) triple your sales without any additional effort!

More importantly, Amazon rewards conversion. If Amazon detects that a book is suddenly converting better, it'll promote it more. As we'll see in the section dedicated to the retail giant, Amazon's goal is to sell books. So if their system has to choose between featuring two different books in a promo e-mail, which book do you think they'll choose? The highest-converting one.

Ninety percent of the time, when an author comes to me for marketing guidance, there's something wrong with their funnel. Or at the very least, something that could be greatly improved. The first step in book marketing is not bringing traffic; it's improving conversion. And that's why all the chapters in this section are dedicated to dissecting the steps of the funnel, one by one, and offering you practical tips for crafting a product and packaging that readers in your niche just can't help but buy.

10

Cover design rules

So *much* advice about cover design already exists (including on the Reedsy blog) that it's impossible to write a chapter about the topic without repeating most of what is readily available online. And at the same time, I can't afford to include a chapter on cover design without mentioning all of that vital advice you probably already know about. So I'll repeat it, starting with the golden rule of cover design.

Golden rule: Do not design your book covers yourself

Now, I know this is controversial advice. I know many authors have done well with self-made covers. And I know not everyone has the budget to commission professional covers for a whole series. (Remember: you should write in series.) So I'll add some caveats below, but I don't want to blur or tarnish this golden rule, simply because I have seen too many horrendous self-made covers.

See, every few months we run what we call a "Reedsy cover critique" event. We invite authors to submit their book covers (whether they've created those themselves or worked with a professional designer), and select a shortlist of twenty or more to be critiqued live in a webinar by a professional artist from the Reedsy Marketplace.

These events are a great way to learn about cover design, but what they've taught me is that far too many authors still think they can do their covers themselves.

After all, authors are creatives, right? So they have a ton of ideas about *what* the cover should look like. Plus, who better than the author knows what happens in the book, and all the oh-so important elements that absolutely need to be reflected on the cover?

And there's the catch: the objective of a book cover is not to make the author happy or to accurately represent what happens in the book; it's to make the relevant reader want to buy. That is the one and only goal of the cover. It doesn't matter if the cover features a character who has a slightly different hair color than the character in your book. It doesn't matter if it doesn't include the tiny details you think are vital to the plot. It only matters if it catches the eyes of readers in your niche and makes them want to buy the book.

Authors are often too close to their story, their characters, and the tiny details to design such a cover. More importantly, they often lack the graphic design expertise. And this is not something you pick up in a day—just like writing a book is not something you pick up in a book.

So please, pretty please, do not design your books' covers yourself, unless:

1. You have a lot of *professional* graphic design experience. (By that I mean you have previously made a living as a graphic designer.)
2. You have absolutely no budget to invest in your book. I'm not saying "to invest in your cover," because I think your cover is the number-one thing you should spend money on (perhaps tied with editing).

And if you *do* design it yourself—either because you're in one of the two cases above or because you've chosen to ignore this golden rule—then at least please follow the silver rule below.

Silver rule: Carefully research cover trends and expectations in your niche

Let's face it: in many fiction genres, readers expect to see specific elements on a cover—just like they expect to encounter specific genre tropes in the story.

Think about it:

- In a romance, you almost always need a happily-ever-after ending.
- In a young adult epic fantasy, you almost always want to model your plot on the hero's journey.
- Police procedurals almost always end with the detective putting together the clues and discovering whodunnit.

These are all genre expectations. If your book doesn't meet them, it'll likely disappoint readers.

Apply this to cover design and the questions become: Does my urban fantasy cover need a character with flaming hands? Does my thriller cover need a dark setting with pines? Does my shifter romance need an animal?

More often than not, the answer to these questions can be found by simply looking at the books that do well in these categories. In 2020 Reedsy did just that by manually reviewing twenty Amazon fiction subcategories and analyzing the commonalities among the covers of the top one hundred books in each of these categories.[11] We found out some compelling things; for example:

- More than 90 percent of covers in the Urban Fantasy top one hundred use a serif font for the title.
- Sixty five percent of covers in the Space Opera top one hundred feature a spaceship, and 40 percent feature an alien planet. (Many feature both.)
- Eighty percent of covers in the Animal Cozy Mystery top one hundred are illustrated (vs. using photo manipulation).

These examples are what I mean when I talk about genre expectations. If your space opera book doesn't feature a spaceship or a planet (or both), it'll likely send the wrong signal to readers in that genre (i.e., that your book doesn't belong there).

You'll find a link to that 2020 analysis in the endnotes, but if your genre is not covered in it, you can simply replicate our methodology on your own for the categories of your choice.

Of course, trends and expectations change. That's why authors (and publishers) often redesign their covers every few years to follow new trends, revive the backlist, and test different designs. Speaking of testing … here's the bronze rule!

Bronze rule: Testing cover designs

If you hire a professional artist to design your cover (well done!), they'll probably come up with several cover concepts for you to choose from. At that stage, most authors pick one based on what *they* like best, i.e., based on intuition. But your instinctual choice is not necessarily the one that will work best to attract the right readers to the book.

And that's where testing comes into play: instead of making vital decisions based on intuition, you run a simple test. When you get your cover concepts from the designer, you use them to create a basic Facebook ad:

- First, make sure to target a close comparative author in your genre.
- Then set up identical ads on Facebook, each with a different cover concept (but all with the exact same text and call to action).

Once the ads have garnered enough impressions, check their click-through rate. The ad with the highest click-through rate will be the one whose cover is the most attractive to readers in your genre—which is what really matters at the end of the day.

This is something we've always tried to push at Reedsy because, frankly, we don't see a lot of authors doing it—or doing it well. In 2017, we ran a little experiment: we offered to redesign the covers of four indie books and then ran a test on Facebook, pitting the old covers against the new. You'll find a link to a post detailing the experiment and the results in the endnotes,[12] but spoiler alert: all four new covers had a higher click-through rate than the previous designs.

Now, this test isn't foolproof—you're only testing the click-through rate, not the conversion rate—but it should be enough to tell you which cover is most effective at attracting readers in your genre.

Of course, if you already have a big mailing list of engaged readers, then you can simply ask them which cover they prefer. Keep in mind, though, that your existing readers will be *biased*. They'll already be familiar with—and attached to—your brand. So their opinion will likely differ from that of an *unbiased* group of readers (like those you'd reach through Facebook ads).

Your cover is your single most important marketing tool, so don't be afraid to spend a few extra bucks on ads to make sure you get it *just right* for your genre.

11

Blurb-writing tips

Imagine spending countless solitary hours writing the perfect 80,000-word book, only to have someone say, "Can you just sum it up for me in a couple of paragraphs?"

Surely that person would become the unfortunate victim of a dreadful murder in your next book.

But the problem is, it's not a person asking you to reduce your book to fewer than a dozen sentences. It's Amazon. And Kobo. And Apple. And, well, any place where you may hope to sell your book.

After the cover, the blurb

Book descriptions, or blurbs, are the second most important element in the conversion funnel. If a reader is sufficiently intrigued by your cover to click on your book—or pick it up from a shelf—what are they going to do next? Read the blurb. Their decision to either purchase the book or put it back on the shelf hangs on how much they enjoy this blurb and whether they want to find out more. The importance of these few short paragraphs is matched only by how damn hard they are to write!

The most common blurb-writing mistakes

Now, I'm not a great blurb writer myself, and it's definitely not something I enjoy, either. So instead of sharing my advice on book blurbs, I'll leave you with that of someone far more experienced than me: Victoria Jacobi from our Reedsy Discovery team.

* * *

At Discovery I skim authors' blurbs every day and often need to rewrite them when pitching books to reviewers. So where do they go wrong? Usually they feature at least one of four mistakes:

- They introduce too many story elements.
- The blurb is a review in disguise.
- There are no stakes.
- The description is too generic.

Avoiding these pitfalls is easier said than done, especially in your own blurb. So let's take a look at how these mistakes might look for a book most of you have probably read: *Harry Potter and the Sorcerer's Stone*.

1. They introduce too many story elements

> *"Harry Potter grew up with his mother's family after his parents passed away when he was a baby. Receiving little attention and affection underneath the Dursley roof, Harry can't believe his luck when he is sent a letter. But his aunt and uncle do not want him to read it."*

Readers need to instantly know what a book will be about, the key word being *instantly*. Are we focusing on the family dynamic? Finding out about the secret letter? Of course Harry Potter is about both of these things, but neither is the main plot.

Let's take a look at the story elements we've introduced here:

- Backstory of his parent's death
- Relationship between Harry and his family
- Mysterious letter

Not only are you wasting important real estate in the first three lines, but you're leaving little breathing room for curiosity, shoving all these story elements down a reader's throat.

```
How to spot the problem: Ask yourself for each sentence in the
blurb: Is this my main plotline? Does it directly relate to it?
```

2. The blurb is a review in disguise

"For fans of Narnia, Harry Potter is an enthralling tale of witchcraft and wizardry, featuring a flying motorcycle, a troll in the dungeon, and a magical castle. Appealing to both young and mature readers, this is the perfect book for bedtime reading!"

I know where authors are coming from with this approach. Best-selling books feature glowing reviewer and author quotes. But the crucial difference is that these reviews and quotes are not the blurb. Your job as an indie author is not to review your own book. If your cover has caught the reader's attention, what they want to know is: Who will they be spending time with? What is at stake?

```
How to spot the problem: Are you using value adjectives such as
"delightful" or "captivating"? Have you introduced your main
character? Have you introduced the stakes?
```

Which brings us to the next point...

3. There are no stakes

"Harry is just a normal boy until he discovers he can use magic. He is summoned to attend a prestigious yet secret wizarding school, and an unforgettable adventure begins."

A sequence of events is not a story. Where is the conflict? What is at risk for Harry? Harry is living a miserable life in a cupboard underneath the stairs until he discovers his magical powers. Now we've at least introduced some stakes to the first sentence: escaping a miserable life. Always put an event into the context of what is at risk for the protagonist.

```
How to spot the problem: Ask yourself: what is at stake for my
protagonist, and does my blurb make this clear?
```

4. The description is too generic

"When Harry finds out he's a wizard, he's catapulted into a secret magical world. But dark forces lurk in the shadows—can Harry win the fight against evil?"

This blurb gives me the same vibe as a telemarketing company trying to scam me into a new phone rate. Don't get me wrong; it's quite punchy and creates some excitement. But the "novice" and "dark vs. evil" tropes are about as fresh as the lost sock underneath your sofa. Who or what are the dark forces? What kind of fight are we talking about? You've got a unique and original story to tell; don't sell yourself short!

```
How to spot the problem: Is your blurb just a few lines, and/or
does it feature one common trope after another? Have you added
details to your character? Are you showing what's unique about
your story?
```

If you take away one thing from these mistakes, make it this: identify the central question that drives your story and make sure people are left asking that question after reading your blurb.

* * *

With these tips in mind (thanks, Victoria!), you should be able to write a blurb that avoids the most common mistakes; introduces your main characters, the conflict, and the stakes; and makes the reader want to immediately open the book. And if you need more tips, you'll find a whole blog post in the endnotes about writing novel blurbs.[13]

"But what about us nonfiction authors?" You're right, most of the advice above caters almost exclusively to fiction and narrative nonfiction authors. But there's a reason for that: Writing blurbs is generally much harder for fiction than for nonfiction. For a reference or how-to book, the blurb should simply sum up the main message of your book. It takes some copywriting skills, too, but if your book is well-structured, tackles a clear problem, and has a well-identified target audience, then the blurb should almost write itself.

Use HTML formatting... sparingly

Most online retailers will allow you to format your blurb using HTML formatting. This is a great way to make some elements of your blurb stand out or to present your blurb in the most readable way.

For example, you could:

· Use bold or header formatting to make your first sentence hook pop.
· Use italics to highlight a quote or short editorial review.

Look inside ↓

The John Milton Series: Books 1-3 (The John Milton Series Boxset Book 1) Kindle Edition
by Mark Dawson ∨ (Author)   Format: Kindle Edition
☆☆☆☆☆ ∨   2,874 ratings
Book 1 of 5: John Milton

› See all formats and editions

Kindle	Paperback
from $7.99	$25.99
Read with Our Free App	4 Used from $18.47
	2 New from $20.20

The first three thrillers in the million-selling John Milton series: The Cleaner, Saint Death and The Driver.

"It's impossible not to think of Lee Child's super-selling Jack Reacher. " - The Times

· In nonfiction, use bullet points to showcase the main messages or learning points from the book.

That said, you should not turn your blurb into an HTML festival. If you add header, bold, italics, and underline formatting all over it, it will not only become unreadable, but also look particularly scammy.

If you're familiar with HTML code, then you can simply add it to the book description box when you upload your book to the relevant retailers. If you're not, then you'll find a book description generator in the endnotes[14] that will generate all the code for you. It works for Amazon, Barnes & Noble and Kobo, the three main e-retailers that support HTML formatting on book descriptions.

Work in the right keywords... without stuffing

Some online retailers will scan your blurb and use it to index your book for relevant searches. (I'll discuss this more in depth in the next two sections.) So it's a good idea to work in relevant keywords as long as they're *related to your genre*. For example, if you write a terrorism thriller, you might want to include the keywords "FBI," "spy," "bomb," "terrorist—if these elements actually feature in your book.

What you don't want to do, however, is artificially stuff your blurb with keywords. This is not an Instagram post. You don't need a section with hashtags or keywords, and most stores will automatically ask you to edit them out if you add them.

The main objective of the blurb is to turn readers who come across your book into customers. Including a few relevant keywords will help somewhat with discoverability, but it should *never* be at the expense of the readability of the blurb.

As you can imagine, juggling all these different elements and finding the right balance is rarely easy, which begs the question …

Can I get someone else to do it for me?

Blurb writing is one of those activities I don't always recommend authors outsource: you're a writer, and no one knows your book better than you.

That said, copywriting *is* an entirely different skill from writing a novel, so if the idea of writing that book description is too daunting—or if your book isn't selling and you suspect your blurb might be a cause—then do consider hiring someone to (re)write it for you. Blurb changes, like cover redesigns, have proven remarkably successful at resurrecting dead books.

Authors are often tempted to ask their editors to help them write the blurb. After all, your editor is probably the second person who knows your book best. But unless your editor has proven copywriting skills, I'd wager they're not the best person to write your blurb.

Instead, I'd suggest you hire *a marketer.* Blurb writing is not so much about creative writing as it is about marketing. We have a few verified book marketers on Reedsy who specialize in blurb writing and Amazon metadata—you can find them in the marketing section of our Marketplace, under "Metadata & Blurb Optimization." (You'll need to sign up or log in first.)

Blurbs, like covers, can be easily tested via Facebook ads. Just run two identical ads to the same audience, each featuring a different version of your blurb, and see which one gets the highest click-through rate.

After the cover and the blurb, the next step in the conversion funnel is reviews. That's what we'll talk about next—and because they're such a thorny issue, we'll need several chapters to discuss them.

12

Just how important are reviews?

I see a lot of confusion and myths out there about book reviews. The biggest one, probably, is that Amazon reviews directly influence your book's position in the rankings and lists. That myth has been proven untrue time and again.

Amazon reviews influence only *one* thing: how readers perceive your book when they come across it. In other words, reviews aren't a factor of *discoverability*. They're a factor of *conversion*.

Bearing that in mind, what about reviews *does* matter? Getting as many reviews as possible? Getting only positive reviews? Getting in-depth reviews? Getting reviews from famous people?

Let's put on our reader hats for a moment. When you visit a book's page on Amazon, what do you look for in the reviews? Personally, I tend to look at:

- The number of reviews. The more reviews a book has, the more *successful* it appears. It's a basic element of social validation, like likes on a Facebook post or YouTube video.
- Featured (top) reviews. Amazon ranks reviews based on when they were published (newer reviews get more prominence) and how many other readers upvoted them as "helpful." Generally, only the first two to ten reviews will show up on the book's page.

The issue of top reviews is too often overlooked. See, if all your five-stars reviews are basic "loved this book," "a great story," "definite must-read" platitudes, then as soon as someone posts a sensible two-star review with a couple of paragraphs, that review will likely get more upvotes than all your five-star reviews, which means it will show up first on your book's page. Here's an example, taken from a book with more than eight hundred reviews and an average of 4.3 out of five stars:

☆☆☆☆☆ **From good to worse**
Reviewed in the United States on November 13, 2015
Verified Purchase

The free preview made me think that I was really going to like this book and for the first third of it, I was having a good time. The character development for Charlie was really working and I found myself rooting for the scrappy young thief. The world-building was going well and I was looking forward to seeing what happened. Then everything went wrong.

First, Charlie turned into a bad romance character rather than a good urban fantasy character. Despite being kidnapped and beaten, she decided that the man who was holding her was just so dreamy and couldn't stop thinking about how manly he was. This guy, who is being forced into the position of eventual love interest for no reason that I could perceive, kidnaps her, allows her to be attacked and nearly raped in order to gain her loyalty (yeah, still having problems with that), is cold toward her, and for some reason, all of this just makes him super-duper appealing to her.

And then there was how when she was disguised as a boy, she was smart and persistent while trying to fight back and escape. Once she was "womanized," she became pretty much useless. She was either a hostage or kidnap-bait.

⌄ Read more

221 people found this helpful

| Helpful | Comment | Report abuse |

☆☆☆☆☆ **Disappointing shift from fantasy story to distasteful romance**
Reviewed in the United States on July 9, 2016
Verified Purchase

Based on the free sample of this story, I was intrigued--a woman posing as a young boy in order to get buy, necromancy powers that she has never really explored, and people trying to track her down because of those powers for unknown reasons. I enjoyed the first third of the book, where we saw Charlie struggling to find a way to deal with her situation, but the romance really killed it for me, and a number of the twists later on in the story were predictable. The story presented opportunities for Charlie to develop meaningful and interesting relationships, not just in the romantic category but through friendships and working relationships with the other main characters, but only a few of these were actualized. Worse, the "romance" was both predictable and not appealing because of how

It might seem unfair, but because these two reviews are long and have received the most "helpful" upvotes, they are effectively burying all the other positive reviews.

Not all reviews are created equal

All of this is to say: it's not just about numbers. The *quality* of the reviews matters. One positive review that goes in depth into why the reviewer liked your book is worth more than a hundred positive reviews that consist of generic "loved it!" one-liners. This is not only because it'll get more "helpful" upvotes and therefore show up first on Amazon, but because you'll also be able to use an excerpt from it for your book description, or even for ads.

A well-written, meaningful, positive review is an element of social validation that can greatly improve your conversion and turbocharge your ads. This is what the concept of Reedsy Discovery is all about: using meaningful reviews to help promote books to readers.

So, how do you get such a review? Well, we keep a free, up-to-date directory of book review bloggers open to submissions,[15] which is always a good place to start. If a reviewer has a blog, it means they're serious about reviewing and will probably write a review with more *meat* than your average reader. The downside is that most reviewers are already swamped under submissions, so you'll need to make sure you reach out to them well in advance of your launch.

Now, even if I said it's not *just* about numbers, I don't mean that numbers don't matter. A high number of reviews (in the hundreds) conveys the idea that the book has sold quite well and that readers have enjoyed it. A number in the thousands indicates a best seller. And a book with just one or two reviews is ... well, the opposite of that: for many readers, it's equivalent to a sign saying, "Read at your own risk."

Which is why you need to make sure that every book you launch gathers a good number of reviews (at least twenty) in the first few days after the launch.

13

Building your street team

Getting reviews is often seen as a chicken-and-egg problem, since you need sales to get reviews, but you also need reviews to convince people to buy your book. So how can one get reviews before publication? The answer is simple: you need a street team.

What's a street team? It's a group of dedicated readers, ultra-fans of your writing, with whom you have a special agreement: they get to read your books in advance and for free—you send them advance reader copies, or ARCs—and in exchange they commit to leaving you an *honest* review at launch. Often, street team members can serve as beta readers as well, meaning they offer feedback on your writing and help you catch the typos and errors your editors didn't.

Rules for the street team

Here are a few things to keep in mind when you start to build your street team:

- Keep your street team separate from your main mailing list. If you use an e-mail marketing provider, you'll want to have at least two different lists.
- Interact with your street team in between launches (especially if you're

61

not a fast writer). Offer them sneak peeks at what you're working on, tell them about your life, do cover reveals, run exclusive giveaways, etc.
- Don't hesitate to send them a few e-mails close to your launch to remind them to leave a review, and an e-mail a week after launch telling them how your book's doing and reminding them to post a review if they haven't already.
- Tell your street team to *always* mention in their reviews that they received an ARC from the author. Otherwise, Amazon might delete the review.
- I recommend using BookFunnel to deliver advance reader copies to your street team in their preferred format. This service will take care of the delivery and customer support, and save you a lot of time and hassle.

Now, let's get to the main question you're probably wondering: *"Where do I find people for my street team?"*

Finding your first street team members

Well, you probably know a few friends who've read and enjoyed your books, right? Start there. And then make other friends in your genre! Reach out to other authors you like and ask if they're looking for more beta readers. If you join their street team and regularly interact with them, chances are they'll return the favor.

Writer conferences are also a great place to meet and make friends with fellow writers. Face-to-face interaction is all the more valuable in an increasingly digital world.

Finally, you can find beta readers and street team members on social media. We have a Reedsy Facebook group called "The Street Team"[16] dedicated to just that. Simply post a few lines about your book and ask if anyone would like to become a beta reader.

Growing your street team

Once you have a solid street team of, say, twenty or thirty dedicated readers, you can easily keep growing it by regularly inviting your main list subscribers to join it.

For example, if you have an automation workflow for new mailing list subscribers (don't worry, I'll explain what that is in the mailing list section of this book), you could set up an e-mail after a week or two that only goes to the most engaged subscribers (readers who opened and clicked through on previous e-mails) and tells them about your street team.

Make your expectations clear: if they join, they commit to reading your ARCs before launch and leaving a review at launch. Your goal is to build a bridge between your two mailing lists, but to make sure only true fans cross over.

Now, not everyone is a big fan of the street team—it does mean you're giving up on a good number of almost-guaranteed sales at launch, since you're giving them the book for free—but it's the single most effective way to get a ton of reviews just a few days after launch. And that often makes up for the lost sales, because customer reviews are a natural conversion booster.

14

What about editorial reviews?

So far, I've been referring mostly to consumer reviews—i.e., reviews from random readers who buy your book or get it free as part of an advance reader copy team.

But a customer review isn't the only kind of review. For example, editorial reviews are authored by professional or semiprofessional reviewers. These are posted on blogs or websites other than Goodreads, Amazon, or other e-retailers.

The most popular examples of editorial reviews are the ones you'll find in newspapers or online magazines like the *New York Times*, the *New York Review of Books* or the *Washington Post*.

Now, these are the dream of many an author—but the actual value of these famous editorial reviews is doubtful, and certainly not worth the effort. As an indie author, you'd have to find a *very* expensive publicist to have a remote chance of getting your book reviewed on those outlets.

To give you an example, in 2016 Mark Thompson, the former CEO of the *New York Times*, released his book, *Enough Said*, which, oh, surprise, got a review in the *NYT*. Guess how many copies that book ended up selling? According to a source: under one thousand. Right now, it has fewer than forty reviews on the Amazon US store.

I've attended conferences with hundreds of indie authors who will never get reviews in the *NYT*—and whose books sell ten times better.

"So are all editorial reviews worthless?" Definitely not.

First, countless indie book bloggers have strong, engaged audiences in niche genres—and many of them are open to reviewing indie books. Of course, it'll require a bit of work on your part to get your book reviewed: you need to research each book blog in depth, pitch your book elegantly (and well in advance), follow up, and so on.

Whether that's worth your time is up for you to decide, but it's certainly an avenue worth considering, especially if you don't have an established readership. To help you with that, remember we have an always up-to-date directory of the best book bloggers on the internet, which you'll find in the bonus resources of this book.

More importantly, even if an editorial review doesn't yield *direct* sales, it's a fantastic tool to use for your other marketing efforts.

Editorial reviews tend to be written much better than your average random customer review, making them a lot more quotable. You can reuse such quotes in your book description, back-cover copy, advertising copy—you get the picture.

A quote from a recognized source in your genre will carry *a lot* more weight in the eyes of readers than one from "Anonymous Amazon Customer."

Which brings me to ...

Reedsy Discovery

If you're not already aware of it, Reedsy Discovery is a product we launched in 2018 that seeks to bring together authors, editorial reviewers, and readers on one platform—therefore making editorial reviews that much more meaningful and useful.

See, while *some* indie book bloggers have big audiences and can drive sales to the books they positively review, most of them don't. Besides, the ones with sizable audiences are flooded with submissions from the big publishers, which means it's that much harder for you to get your indie book in the door.

Our goal with Discovery is to create a common place for every party. By posting their reviews on Discovery, book reviewers (whom we strictly vet) get access to our growing audience of readers. In return, these readers get access to a selection of the best indie books, curated and reviewed by semiprofessional reviewers in their preferred niche. And authors can get their books reviewed by reviewers *and* get their books in front of our readers.

Now, Reedsy Discovery is only for unpublished or newly released books. So if you have a new release coming up, think about submitting it to Discovery! It'll only cost you fifty dollars, and (as a reward for reading this book thus far) you can use the coupon code "RICARDO" at checkout to get ten dollars off.

Just be aware of the risk factor associated with submitting to Discovery. First, we can't guarantee your book will be reviewed: it doesn't depend on us, and we can't force reviewers on our platform to pick up your book if they don't want to. That said, around 70 percent of submitted books *are* getting reviewed right now—and you can imagine the covers of those that don't. (Did I mention you should *hire a professional cover designer?*)

Second, it's not guaranteed that you'll get a positive review—it would make for a terrible experience for readers if every book on Discovery had five stars. But even a three-star review will be mostly positive and will have quotable excerpts you can use in your ads, on your retailer product pages, or even on your cover.

Speaking of which, the next chapter is all about that: cover quotes.

15

Getting cover quotes

I was on a panel in 2018 during which an author asked us for our number-one piece of marketing advice. This was around when Michael Wolff's *Fire and Fury* was topping the charts following Trump's comments about it. So my good friend and fellow panelist, Dan Wood from Draft2Digital, came up with a perfect answer: "Get the President of the United States to trash your book."

Aside from the joke, there's a pretty good lesson here—and it's not "There's no such thing as bad press," because there is. No, the lesson is that one of the best ways to sell a book is to get someone with an established platform in your genre or topic to talk about it—and ideally to recommend it.

This is an area where the big publishers are actually quite skilled. Whenever they prepare the release of a new book, the first thing they do is get cover quotes or blurbs from established authors or influencers. For example, here's a marketing case study from the Goodreads blog for *The Silent Patient*, the first book published by the Macmillan imprint Celadon Books:

> *"The Celadon team started promoting* The Silent Patient *in February 2018, an entire year before publication (in February 2019). As Alex Michaelides is a debut author, they knew blurbs would play an important role. The team's first step, therefore, was to ask popular*

thriller authors to read the book and provide quotes. They got the first hint of just how big the book could be when rave blurbs came back from best-selling authors Lee Child, David Baldacci, Douglas Preston, Lincoln Child, A.J. Finn, and Blake Crouch."

So how are these blurbs used? Well, the most prestigious one is generally featured on the cover (a cover quote), while the others can be featured in the book's blurb and back-cover copy:

WITH OVER A MILLION COPIES SOLD, read the *Sunday Times* and No.1 *New York Times* bestselling, record-breaking thriller that everyone is talking about - soon to be a major film.

'The perfect thriller' **AJ FINN**

'Terrific' - **THE TIMES Crime Book of the Month**

'Smart, sophisticated suspense' - **LEE CHILD**

'Compelling' - **OBSERVER**

'Absolutely brilliant' - **STEPHEN FRY**

'A totally original psychological mystery' - **DAVID BALDACCI**

'One of the best thrillers I've read this year' - **CARA HUNTER**

Book description of The Silent Patient

As you can imagine, this is the ultimate conversion rate booster, as it gives instant credibility to an otherwise unknown author.

Accessing midlevel influencers

"Sure, but that's easy for publishers: they can get the big names to read and review any book they want."

True, but there's influencer, and then there's *influencer*. If you're self-publishing a political nonfiction book, you probably won't be able to get Obama or Trump to praise (or criticize) it. But you might be able to get a quote from a local political figure.

If you're writing your debut thriller, you'll probably never hear back from

Lee Child or James Patterson. But with the *right strategy*, you might be able to get a big indie author (think Mark Dawson, Adam Croft, or Diane Capri) or an Amazon Publishing author (like Robert Dugoni) to give you a quote. After all, it's great publicity for them to have their name featured on another author's cover!

In other words, you don't need to shoot for the stars. What matters is that the influencer who writes your blurb is popular enough that people in your niche know or have heard of them.

Building relationships

So what does this "right strategy" look like? Here's how I'd go about it.

1. Create a list of prospects

First, you need to identify potential influencers. My guess is you already know who the influential authors and influencers are in your genre, so start there. Then think about other mediums:

- Are there any famous book review blogs in your genre?
- Are there any podcasts your readers listen to?
- Are there any YouTubers who regularly cover your genre?
- Are there any Instagram influencers whom you think a majority of your target market follows?

Try to be as exhaustive as possible in your research. Then be as *selective* as possible when filtering out prospects. You want to get down to a list of two or three people, the ones you *really, really* want to get a blurb from.

2. Build a relationship

For the top influencers on your list, a simple e-mail probably won't cut it. Instead, spend some time acquainting yourself with their work and engaging with them through social media.

For example, if they're an author:

- Read as many of their books as you can and review them.
- Engage with them through Twitter, or join their Facebook reader group.
- Subscribe to their newsletter and answer some of their e-mails.

If they're an Instagram or YouTube influencer, follow them on that medium and comment regularly (without seeming like a creepy stalker). The goal is for them to get to know you as a fan of their work. Become a name they'll recognize when it appears in their e-mail inbox.

Obviously, this is time-consuming, which is why I don't recommend you do it for everyone on your list.

```
Pro tip: The best way to build a real relationship is to meet
them in person--which is what conferences are for! Most of the
best relationships I've built in publishing have been through
conferences.
```

3. When the time comes, ask for that blurb

Don't do it out of the blue, though. If you're a new or unpublished author, let them know early on that you're working on your first book. If you've already published a few books, hint at that in your conversations and comments.

Then, a few months before you release the book, ask them if they'd be open to reading it and (if they like it) offering a sentence or two that you could feature on your blurb or cover. Sweeten the deal by sending them a proper paperback if they agree.

I know this might seem like a lot of effort just to get *one* review. But that review can have such a positive impact on all your other marketing efforts that it can often be worth it, especially if you're a first-time author.

This closes the section on conversion! If there's anything you take away from it, it should be these three points:

1. Hire a professional cover designer *with experience in your niche* to design your books' covers.
2. Learn about copywriting and write, rewrite, and re-rewrite your blurb until you nail it. Or save yourself time and hire a professional marketing copywriter to write it for you.
3. Build a street team of at least twenty to thirty people committed to leaving an honest review on every new book you launch.

Once all these conversion elements are polished to perfection, it's time to start thinking about how you'll bring *traffic* to your book pages. All the following chapters will focus on different ways to achieve that.

IV

Amazon marketing

In 2019, Amazon's CEO, Jeff Bezos, announced that more than one thousand indie authors were earning in excess of $100,000 a year through Kindle Direct Publishing. While Amazon is not the only retailer for books, it is unquestionably the dominant one—with more than 85 percent market share for e-books and more than 40 percent for print books in the US and UK.
So if you're going to make a living self-publishing, you'll need to first learn their rules and understand their algorithms.

16

The guiding principles of Amazon algorithms

Disclaimer: A large portion of the content you'll find in this section is taken from the Reedsy Learning course I wrote titled "Everything You Need to Know about Amazon Algorithms." So if you've already taken the course, don't be surprised! But also, don't skip this section—not only will it refresh your memory, I've also incorporated several bits throughout that you'll only find in this book.

The first thing to highlight when talking about Amazon algorithms is the *plural* in algorithms. See, Amazon uses more than one algorithm to rank and display books on their store. They use a combination of several different algorithms that impact different areas in the Amazon store. So here's a first word of caution: you'll find a plethora of gurus who claim to know the secret of "The Amazon Algorithm." And believe it or not, they'll be ready to let you in on their closely guarded secret ... provided you purchase their four-figure course, of course.

So don't listen to anyone talking about *the* algorithm. They'll be, at best, misinformed, and more often than not trying to sell you an expensive course, coaching session, or webinar.

Now, I can already imagine your question: what the heck is an "algo-rithm"? Well, when it comes to search engines and retail sites, an algorithm is a set of rules and calculations a computer follows to *rank and display* results and products.

Google is famous, for example, for their RankBrain algorithm, which decides which results to show you when you google something, as well as the ranking of these results.

Amazon's algorithms, similarly, decide which books show up, and in what order, for searches performed by their users on the store. For example, if I search for "epic fantasy series," Amazon currently returns a list of more than twenty thousand results. The books that show up, and their order, is decided by their search algorithm (also called the A9 algorithm, which we'll get to later).

But more than that, other Amazon algorithms also decide the ranking of books on Best Seller lists as well as the placement of books in recommendation e-mails. If you've ever browsed Amazon as a reader, I'm sure you've received an e-mail at some point recommending books to you. These recommendations are selected by an algorithm.

With sales come more sales

While Amazon has different algorithms, they all share the same philosophy, which is also the philosophy of Amazon itself: keep readers happy and get them to *buy as many books as possible*. It's an important yet often disregarded point that Amazon's goal is the same as yours: selling books. The more books they sell, the more money they make. What *you* want is for them to sell your book—and that's what this whole chapter is about.

Following this philosophy, the number-one factor in algorithm computations on Amazon is *sales*. The more copies your book sells on Amazon, the more prominent Amazon will make it on their store and in their e-mails.

Sustained sales vs. spikes

All sales are not created equal, though. For example, if you land a BookBub deal and your sales skyrocket for a day before going back to normal, Amazon will see this spike as an anomaly and won't reward these sales as much as if they had occurred over several days of a sustained sales level increase.

In other words, Amazon favors plateaus over sales spikes:

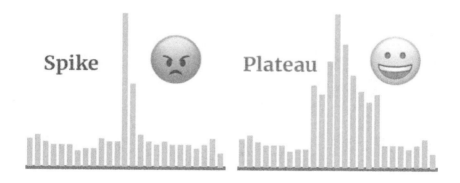

On top of *when* they happen, it's also important to consider *where* the sales come from. For example, for keyword search results, Amazon will give more importance to full-price sales that come through previous, similar keyword searches from other readers rather than sales that come through external sites. The logic is simple: if Amazon notices your book sells well for a given search, they'll want to bump its prominence for that search.

Which brings us to the second big factor, which is directly related to sales.

The power of conversion

I covered this briefly in the previous section, but it's worth highlighting here again: more than sales, what Amazon rewards is *conversions*.

Why the particular focus on conversion? Because, and I can't stress this enough, *Amazon wants to sell books.* If they have the choice between recommending two books with a similar sales history, Amazon will go for the one with better on-page conversion, because they know the additional traffic they send to that book will turn into more sales.

This is why it's absolutely vital that you spend as much time (and resources) as necessary to nail your Amazon product page—did I mention you should hire a professional to design your cover?

17

Amazon Rank & Popularity Lists

It's time to delve into the technical aspects of Amazon algorithms and how you can optimize your book's visibility on the retail giant.

There are many ways in which Amazon recommends books to readers, and it's important for you as an author to understand how they all play together. In other words, you want to be able to answer this question: how do readers in my genre find new books to read on Amazon?

Amazon Best Sellers lists

The first and most obvious visibility spots are the Best Sellers lists, which readers often browse to know the top sellers on the store.

You'll notice I used the plural here, too, because there are several Best Sellers lists:

- The Kindle Paid Best Sellers list
- The Kindle Free Best Sellers list
- The Print Paid Best Sellers list (which is slightly confusing because it doesn't just include print books, but also best-selling e-books and audiobooks)

While these lists only show the top one hundred books, you can see the rank of any book in the store on its product page, in the Product Details section. This rank is called the Amazon Best Sellers Rank (ABSR), often referred to as "the Rank."

Product details

File Size: 740 KB
Print Length: 288 pages
Publisher: LifeTree Media (April 14, 2020)
Publication Date: April 14, 2020
Sold by: Amazon.com Services LLC
Language: English
ASIN: B084HHX65W
Text-to-Speech: Enabled
X-Ray:
Enabled
Word Wise: Enabled
Lending: Not Enabled
Screen Reader: Supported
Enhanced Typesetting: Enabled
Amazon Best Sellers Rank: #31,688 Paid in Kindle Store (See Top 100 Paid in Kindle Store)
      #12 in Biographies of Social Activists
      #12 in Philanthropy & Charity (Books)
      #4 in Philanthropy & Charity (Kindle Store)

You'll also notice that Amazon displays the Rank of the book in the Best Sellers lists of the main categories in which it is featured. But we'll get to categories in a later chapter.

As their name indicates, the Best Sellers lists are determined only by sales (and Kindle Unlimited borrows), and are believed to be updated on an hourly or daily basis. Since only sales influence Rank, the ABSR is a popular method to *estimate* how well a book is selling.

If you google "Amazon sales rank calculator" you'll find several calculators that will give you an estimate of how many copies a book sells every day based on its Rank. But here's a ballpark chart courtesy of David Gaughran, in his book *Amazon Decoded:*[17]

- #1 to #5 = 5,000+ books a day (sometimes a lot more)
- #5 to #10 = 4,000–5,000
- #10 to #20 = 3,000–4,000

- #20 to #50 = 2,000–3,000
- #100 = 1,000+
- #200 = 500
- #300 = 250
- #500 = 200
- #1,000 = 120
- #2,000 = 100
- #3,000 = 80
- #5,000 = 40
- #10,000 = 20
- #25,000 = 10
- #50,000 = 5
- #100,000+ = fewer than 1 a day

It's important to note that *free downloads* do not count toward Rank. So if you run a free promotion and manage to get 100,000 downloads, you'll likely shoot up to the top of the Kindle Free Best Sellers list. But once your promotion is over, your book will disappear from that list, and its ranking on the Paid list will be unaffected by these downloads.

So are free promotions completely worthless? No, because they are a factor of another, lesser-known algorithm, which is at least as important as the Best Sellers one.

The popularity list

The Popularity list is much harder to find than the Best Sellers lists. First, you need to head to the Kindle eBooks or Amazon Books department on Amazon and then click on the categories that show up in the sidebar—or in the top bar for the cross-format Amazon Books store:

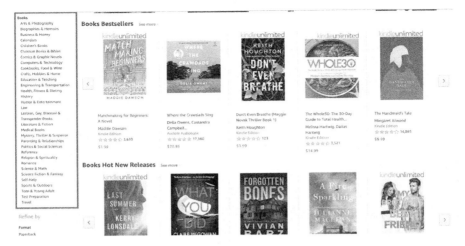

Categories on the Kindle Store

Categories on the cross-format Amazon Books store

When you get to one of these categories, you'll see a number of sections promoting Best Sellers, New Releases, and Highlighted books in that category.

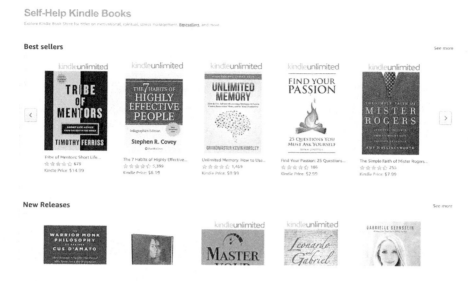

If you scroll further down, though, you'll get to a simple listing of books automatically sorted by "Featured."

In many subcategories, you'll get to that listing immediately. The listing tells you how many books are featured in that category—more than fifty thousand in the screenshot above. And the order of that listing is decided by ... the Popularity list algorithm.

"But why should I even care about the Popularity list when it's so damn hard to find? Surely no one goes through all these steps to find a book on Amazon."

Probably not, but the Popularity list matters because it is the main driver of e-mail recommendations, particularly to Kindle Unlimited subscribers. The Popularity list algorithm is also used by Amazon to order other sections of the store, like the Countdown Deals, and plays a vital part in the ranking of search results for specific keywords.

The Popularity list algorithm

So how are rankings calculated on the Popularity list? First, the Pop list considers a rolling thirty-day average of sales. This means it's much less reactive to spikes than the Best Sellers lists, which (mostly) count sales within the past twenty-four hours.

Then, the Pop list *doesn't factor in* Kindle Unlimited borrows. It does, however, apply a price-weighting coefficient to sales.

"Whoa, wait, what does that mean?"

Imagine that the Popularity algorithm awards points to books based on their sales. A book priced at $4.99 will win more points for each sale than a book priced at $2.99. How many more? We don't know, exactly: the coefficients are probably progressive and changing. But we know higher-priced sales are favored by the Popularity algorithm, while Best Sellers list algorithms are indifferent to price ... unless that price is zero.

Which brings us to the main difference between the Pop and Best Sellers lists: *free downloads count toward rank on the Popularity list.* They don't count as much as a full-price sale (again, there's a price-weighting coefficient); David Gaughran estimates they count as 1/100th of a $2.99 or $3.99 sale.

This may seem tiny, but it's not uncommon to generate fifty thousand or more downloads through a free promotion boosted by a BookBub Featured Deal. This would mean five thousand additional sales, which would be enough to significantly move your book up on the Popularity list.

That move, however, would occur only after a few days. Because—and this is the last peculiarity of the Pop list—there is a four-day lag in recording sales. So after four days, your book would shoot up the Popularity list and would therefore start getting recommended to Kindle Unlimited subscribers.

	Best Sellers Algorithms	Popularity Algorithms
Free downloads	Not counted.	Counted at approximately 1/100th of a full-price sale.
Price weighting	Two books with different prices, but the same amount of sales will have a similar rank.	If two books have the same amount of sales, the one with the higher price will rank much higher.
Page reads	A full Kindle Unlimited borrow is equal to a sale.	Borrows through Kindle Unlimited are not counted.
Immediacy	Sales are recorded immediately.	There is a four-day gap to record a sale or download.

This is why many authors see a big increase in page reads after running a free promotion—often exactly four days after their promotion starts. These page reads, in turn, count toward the Best Sellers rank. And with improved Rank come more sales, closing the virtuous circle of Amazon algorithmic love.

The Best Sellers lists and the Popularity lists are vital because almost everything on the Amazon store is decided by their algorithms. In the next chapter, we'll look at some other visibility spots on the store you should be aware of and analyze how they work—you'll see they're either a result of the Best Sellers or the Popularity algorithms.

18

Hot New Releases, Highly Rated, and Deals

Let's move on and look at a few more places on the Kindle and Books Stores that are heavily trafficked by readers, and therefore important for visibility!

The Hot New Releases list

The Hot New Releases (HNR) list is a subsegment of the Best Sellers list that only accounts for books released within the past thirty days or that are still in preorder. Just like the Best Sellers list and the Pop list, there is an HNR list for every category and subcategory. (Don't worry, the next chapter is all about categories.)

It's often featured on the main Kindle Store home page, and the Best Sellers list of any given category usually features the top three books in its HNR list on the right sidebar. Finally, the HNR list is also a driver of e-mail recommendations. Every time you receive an e-mail from Amazon with "new releases in your genre," it's powered in part by the HNR list.

All of this contributes to making the HNR list a pretty important visibility factor on the store. In fact, you might have heard about the famous "Amazon thirty-day cliff," an expression authors use to describe how their sales suddenly plummet a month after the release.

In recent years, the boost offered by the HNR list has dwindled a bit. I don't think it's due to an algorithm change, though—just increased competition on the store. As more authors release more books, the HNR list will become increasingly competitive. For example, if I look at the Cozy Mystery subcategory, more than 450 books were released in the last thirty days. In the Entrepreneurship one, it's about 370.

HNR list for Cozy Mystery e-books

HNR List for Entrepreneurship e-books

This makes it tough to even land in the top ten of the HNR list in these sub-subcategories.

Highly Rated

While much harder to find on the store, the Highly Rated lists are often featured on the main Kindle eBooks home page, though you might have to scroll down a bit to find them.

Highly Rated
See more

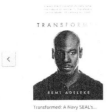

Transformed: A Navy SEAL's...	Socialism Under The Microscope	LEGION RISING: Surviving Combat...	One Friday in Jerusalem: WALKING...
⭐⭐⭐⭐⭐ 457	⭐⭐⭐⭐⭐ 146	⭐⭐⭐⭐⭐ 152	⭐⭐⭐⭐⭐ 125
Kindle Price: $12.81	Kindle Price: $10.38	Kindle Price: $6.10	Kindle Price: $9.58

It's one of the few lists that doesn't rely on the Best Sellers or Popularity algorithms. Instead, Amazon Highly Rated books are simply the books that received the most and best ratings from reviewers on Amazon. It's still unclear exactly how Amazon measures this, but it's believed that more weight is given to verified reviews, recent reviews, and reviews marked as "helpful."

In any case, you can't do much to improve your book's visibility on that list aside from writing a *great* book and assembling a strong street team.

Deals

Kindle Deals are also prominently displayed by Amazon across their store. In my case, they're the first thing I see when I log in to my account and go to the Kindle eBook store.

Deals in History
See more
Up to 80% off select books. These deals run through end of the month.

The Swamp Fox: How Francis Marion Saved the...	Vicksburg: Grant's Campaign That Broke th...	NKJV Study Bible, Full-Color, eBook: The Compl...	How Jesus Became God: The Exaltation of a Jewis...	Misquoting Jesus: The Story Behind Who Chan...
John Oller	Donald L. Miller	Thomas Nelson	Bart D. Ehrman	Bart D. Ehrman
Kindle Edition	Kindle Edition	Kindle Edition	Kindle Edition	Kindle Edition
⭐⭐⭐⭐☆ (424)	⭐⭐⭐⭐☆ (134)	⭐⭐⭐⭐☆ (133)	⭐⭐⭐⭐☆ (703)	⭐⭐⭐⭐☆ (1,154)

There are many types of Kindle Deals, and they all get different levels of visibility:

- Kindle Daily Deals offer the highest level of exposure, but are invite only.
- Kindle Monthly Deals work the same as Kindle Daily Deals, but for a whole month.
- Kindle Exclusive Deals feature books exclusive to Amazon (KDP Select) that are running a limited-time price promo.
- Kindle Countdown Deals are available only to KDP Select authors.

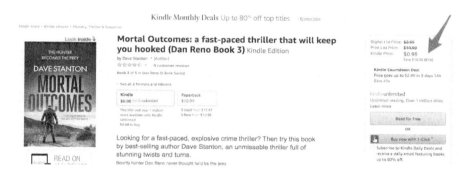

- First-in-series deals feature books that are the first in a series and are temporarily discounted.

Not only are deals prominently featured on the store, they're also a huge driver of e-mail recommendations.

So is it enough to run a Kindle Countdown Deal to start seeing hundreds of sales come in? No, not anymore. And that's for the same reason it's not enough to just launch a new book: the Deals sections have become just as competitive as, if not more than, the Hot New Releases. If you don't actively promote your discount, Amazon won't promote it for you. Luckily, there's a whole section in this book dedicated to price promotions.

19

Amazon categories

I mentioned Amazon categories repeatedly in the past few chapters, and that's because all the lists and visibility spots I highlighted so far exist *in every category* on both the Kindle Store and the Amazon Books store.

For example, there is a:

- Hot New Releases list in Cyberpunk
- Best Sellers list for Health & Nutrition Parenting
- Popularity list for Mysteries & Detectives e-books for children aged 3 to 5
- Etc.

This is crucial because—let's face it—you'll probably never get to the top ten of the Kindle Store Best Sellers list. And if you're a first-time author, you probably also won't be able to compete for the top ten spots of the overall Hot New Releases list.

But even with little preexisting audience and marketing, you can certainly shoot for the top spots of the HNR list in a niche category. This chapter is all about finding these niche categories and getting your book listed under them.

Finding categories

When analyzing categories, it's important to differentiate between the Kindle eBooks store (e-books), and the Amazon Books store (print books), as both have slightly different categories. You can view all the categories by going to the Best Sellers list of both stores and navigating the sidebar:

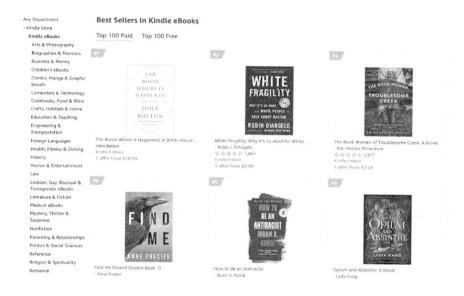

Click on a category to access the subcategories:

‹ Any Department	‹ Any Department	‹ Any Department	Any Department
‹ Kindle Store	‹ Kindle Store	‹ Kindle Store	‹ Kindle Store
‹ Kindle eBooks	‹ Kindle eBooks	‹ Kindle eBooks	‹ Kindle eBooks
Mystery, Thriller & Suspense	‹ Mystery, Thriller & Suspense	‹ Mystery, Thriller & Suspense	‹ Mystery, Thriller & Suspense
Crime Fiction	**Mystery**	‹ Mystery	‹ Mystery
Mystery	African American	**Cozy**	Cozy
Suspense	Amateur Sleuth	Animals	**Animals**
Thrillers	Collections & Anthologies	Crafts & Hobbies	Crafts & Hobbies
	Cozy	Culinary	Culinary
	Hard-Boiled		
	Historical		
	International Mystery & Crime		
	LGBT		
	Police Procedurals		
	Private Investigators		
	Series		
	Traditional Detectives		
	Women Sleuths		

When the sidebar stops offering new subcategories, you've reached the deepest sublevel. And you *want* to list your book in a deep subcategory, because *all the books in a subcategory will show up in its parent category.*

For example, listing your cat cozy mystery only in the huge Mystery, Thriller & Suspense category would be a huge waste because you'd miss out on all the visibility spots offered by the Mystery, Cozy, and Animals Cozy subcategories.

Evaluating categories

Once you've found all the categories that *could* make sense for your book, it's time to analyze them. You want to get a sense of how competitive they are and how much visibility they bring.

The best way to do that is to go through the top five to twenty books in the Best Sellers list of each category and note the Rank of these books.

If the top five books in a category are in the top twenty of the whole store, then you know this is a hyper-competitive category in which you'll probably never reach the top five.

The same goes for the HNR list: you want to make sure your book can get to the top ten of that list when you launch.

At the same time, you also don't want to *only* list your book in super-niche categories, since these won't bring you any visibility. If you see that the number-one book in a category has an ABSR higher than one thousand, you'll know it's a poorly trafficked category.

There are several tools out there that can help save you a lot of time when it comes to category research. My favorite one is Publisher Rocket, and you'll find the link to it in the endnotes.[18] You can also hire a metadata expert on Reedsy to do this for you.[19]

Getting added to the right categories

I recommend selecting anywhere from four to ten deep-level categories where you think your book fits that aren't too competitive or too niche. You'll see in a later chapter why you should *never* list your book in a nonrelevant category.

The tricky part is to get listed in those categories. When you upload your e-book or print book to KDP, you can select *only* two categories, and they don't always match the categories that show up on the store.

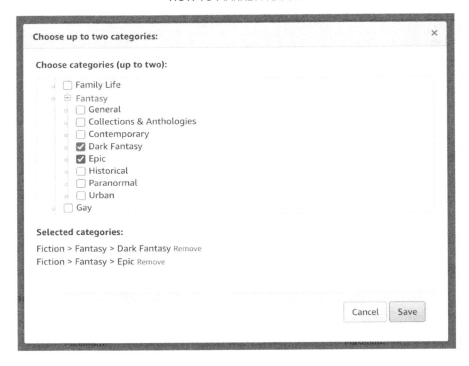

But this doesn't mean your book can only be featured in two categories! First, by using certain keywords, you can get your book automatically included in other categories.

I discuss keywords in more depth in the next chapter, but basically Amazon has some secret "categories with keyword requirements," some of which you can only get featured in if you use a specific keyword in your seven keyword boxes. KDP used to have an easy-to-find page listing all such categories, but it's now hidden. The only way to find it is to google something like "[genre] category keywords"—for example, "science fiction category keywords."

AMAZON CATEGORIES

Science Fiction & Fantasy Keywords

In order for a title to appear in the Science Fiction & Fantasy sub-categories below, the title's search keywords must include at least one of the keywords or phrases listed next to the sub-category. These categories and subcategories are specific to books listed for sale on Amazon.com and Amazon.co.uk; other marketplaces may not support these keywords.

Category	Keywords
Fantasy Characters/Angels	angels
Fantasy Characters/Devils & Demons	demons
Fantasy Characters/Dragons	dragons
Fantasy Characters/Elves & Fae	elf, fae, fairies
Fantasy Characters/Ghosts	ghost, spirit
Fantasy Characters/Gods & Goddesses	deities, god, pantheon
Fantasy Characters/Psychics	psychic, telepathic
Fantasy Characters/Vampires	vampire
Fantasy Characters/Werewolves & Shifters	shapeshifter
Fantasy Characters/Witches & Wizards	witch, wizard, warlock, druid, shaman
Science Fiction Characters/AIs	artificial intelligence
Science Fiction Characters/Aliens	aliens
Science Fiction Characters/Clones	clones
Science Fiction Characters/Corporations	corporations
Science Fiction Characters/Mutants	mutants
Science Fiction Characters/Pirates	pirates, privateer, corsair
Science Fiction Characters/Psychics	psychics
Science Fiction Characters/Robots & Androids	robots, androids
Science Fiction & Fantasy/Horror	horror
Science Fiction & Fantasy/Humor	humor
Science Fiction & Fantasy/Mystery	mystery
Science Fiction & Fantasy/Non-Romantic	Do NOT include "romance" or "love"
Science Fiction & Fantasy/Romantic	romance, love

If you don't want to sacrifice a keyword box just to get into a category, I have some good news for you: you can simply reach out to KDP Support and ask them to add either your print book or e-book (or both) to specific categories on the Kindle or Books store. On the "Contact Us" page, just select "Amazon product page and expanded distribution" then "Update Amazon Categories":

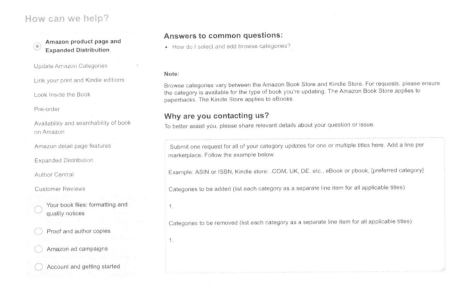

Double-checking your categories

So you've selected your two KDP categories and then reached out to the KDP Help Center to get added to another eight. How do you make sure your book is in the categories you requested?

Previously, Amazon would show you all the categories a book was in, right in the Product Details section, but now it only shows two to four at most. Thankfully, several tools have sprouted up that allow you to easily check what categories any book is listed in. (These tools are also a great way to spy on competitors and find out about potential categories you might have overlooked.) My favorite one is BKLNK:[20] just plug in your ASIN and in one click the tool shows you all the categories that ASIN is listed in.

That's pretty much everything you need to know about categories! Remember:

1. Categories are vital because all the visibility spots we examined in previous chapters exist across all categories.

2. You can get added to as many as ten to twelve categories by reaching out to the KDP Help Center.

3. You *really* don't want to be in a category where your book isn't a perfect fit.

20

Keywords and the A9 algorithm

Amazon is the world's leading search engine for books, and by far. While it's important to know about visibility spots like the Best Sellers, Hot New Releases, and Deals lists, it's equally important to understand how Amazon ranks books in search results.

The A9 algorithm

My answer here is "A9," an algorithm with an actual name (and previously a dedicated website). When you search for "martial arts books" on Amazon, the books that show up in the results, as well as their order, are decided *mostly* by the A9 algorithm.

Indexing for a keyword search

If your book is "indexed" for a keyword, that means it will turn up as a result when a customer enters that term into the Amazon search bar. For example, more than nine thousand e-books are indexed on the Kindle Store for "herbal remedies."

How the A9 algorithm decides which books get indexed for what is determined by three main factors, which I list below by order of importance:

1. Title, subtitle, and series title

It seems obvious: if you have "martial arts" in your title, your book will be indexed for it. This is why a lot of indie authors (and publishers as well) use genre keywords in their titles and add their series title (with more genre keywords) to the book title. For example:

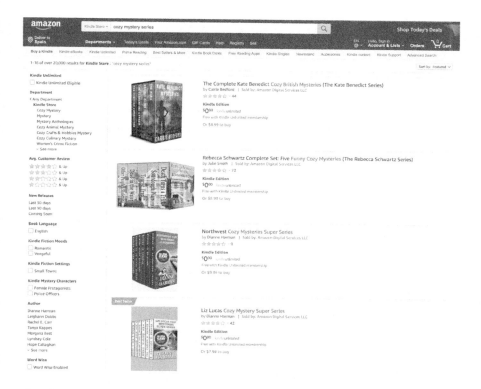

The closer the match between your title, or a part of your title, and the search keyword, the higher your book will rank.

2. The 7 keywords attached to the book

The main purpose of the keywords you select for your e-book or print book on KDP is to tell Amazon what searches your book should appear in. For each keyword, you are allowed up to fifty characters. And Amazon will index your book for *every keyword or string you enter in those fifty characters.*

For example, if one of your keywords is "15th century historical small town mystery," your book will show up for all of the following searches:

- 15th century
- 15th century historical mystery
- Small town mystery
- Historical mystery
- Etc.

Does this mean you should max out your seven keywords with as many characters as possible? Yes and no: Amazon also rewards exact keyword matches. So if you really wanted to rank as high as possible for "15th century mystery," you'd dedicate one of your seven keywords to it.

3. The book description

This indexing factor is a bit trickier. For title and KDP keywords, Amazon will almost always index your book for whatever keywords you use. It won't, however, automatically index your book for every keyword you use in your blurb—far from it.

That said, there is evidence that the A9 algorithm "reads" book descriptions and sometimes uses them for indexing. For example, if I search for "books like Harry Potter" in the Arthurian Fantasy subcategory on the Kindle Store, I get three results indexed. Out of the three, two mention "Harry Potter" in the blurb.

So while you should *never* stuff your book description with keywords, you're certainly encouraged to include relevant genre words (e.g., for an espionage thriller: "spy," "terrorist," "CIA," "vengeance," "intelligence," "murder," "threat," etc.) or mention comparative titles.

Finding and evaluating keyword ideas

So keywords are important, but how do you find and use keywords that have a high search volume?

One way is to use Amazon's autocomplete function in the search bar. Head to the Kindle Store (ideally in an Incognito browser window) and start typing a keyword. You'll see Amazon's autocomplete suggestions:

Amazon has identified these as terms often searched for on the store. These terms therefore make good candidates for your keywords.

While there is no way to know for certain how many monthly searches there are for keywords on Amazon, some pieces of software (like Publisher Rocket) can estimate that figure using the Amazon Best Seller Rank of the top books ranking for that keyword, among other metrics. You should always take their figures with a pinch of salt, but they're certainly a good way to find new keyword ideas.

Back to the Popularity list

"So if I title by book The Ultimate Guide to Martial Arts, *use 'martial arts' as one of my keywords, and use it again in the blurb, I'm sure to rank number one for it, right?"*

No. What we've been talking about so far is *indexing*, not *ranking*. Using the right keywords will allow you to be indexed for the right searches. And in case of exact matches, or inclusion in the title, it might even give you a solid rankings boost. However, the number-one ranking factor for searches is still the same as for everywhere else on Amazon: sales. And in particular, the Popularity list.

So while you can *optimize* your product listing for relevant searches with the right title, keywords, and blurb, your position in the search results will mostly be determined by how your Pop list ranking compares to that of the other books indexed for that keyword.

A last word of warning: *never* optimize your book's pages for keywords not directly related to your book. This is a surefire way to pollute your Also Boughts, and that's the last thing you want.

And if you don't know what "Also Boughts" are, read on.

21

Amazon Also Boughts

I hope you're not tired of hearing about Amazon and how to optimize your book's presence on it. The truth is, I'm fascinated by search engines and how they work. And Amazon's search engine is currently the third most popular one in the world. (I'll let you guess number two.)

But Amazon is more than a search engine. It's a mix between an online store, a search engine, and a *recommendation system*. And that last bit is the most important one.

Dear Amazon, can you recommend me a book?

If there's one thing that hasn't fundamentally changed in the last few years, it's how readers discover new books. Maybe the *places* where they discover books have changed, but the principle behind finding new books has remained the same: it's always been *recommendations*.

How many times have you bought a book because a friend recommended it? How many times have you walked into a physical bookstore and asked the bookseller for recommendations?

Well, believe it or not, Amazon also has a special someone (or in Amazon's case, something) constantly making recommendations to readers. I'll call it *Amazon's internal recommendations system*, or AIRS. (Cute, right?) Have you ever received an e-mail from Amazon recommending you books? That was

AIRS at play. And that is the number-one factor that sells books.

Decrypting Amazon's internal recommendations system

Now, the real question you should be asking is: how do I get featured in one of Amazon's recommendation e-mails? That's kind of a trick question—only God and Amazon know the exact answer. But what we *do* know are the factors that play into the AIRS. Let's break down the two most important ones:

- Your sales (and conversion). No surprise there: your book will only get featured if Amazon sees that it's already doing well.
- Your Also Boughts. These are the books that show up in the section called "Customers who bought this item also bought ..." on your Amazon book page.

Remember: Amazon's number-one goal is to *sell as many books as possible*. So AIRS is looking to promote *hot books* (sales) to *the right audiences* (Also Boughts).

But what are Also Boughts, exactly? Concretely, the Also Boughts of "Book A" on Amazon are the other books customers have bought before or after buying "Book A." In most cases, Amazon will display the "Also Boughts" of a book right below its description:

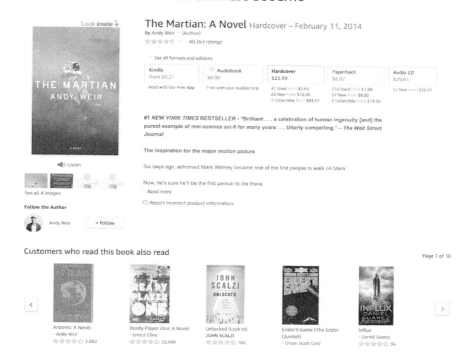

If you use a cool tool like Yasiv.com, you can view all of a book's "Also Bought connections" on the Amazon spider web:

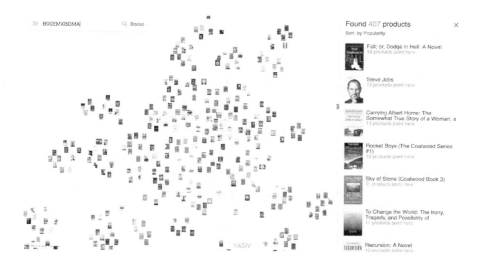

```
Note: As of spring 2020, YASIV is not working anymore, as
Amazon's API rules changed. It might work again in the future,
though.
```

To understand the importance of Also Boughts, just witness what happens when you don't have any—or when the ones you have aren't related to your book.

The proven method for brutally killing your sales

If your book has zero Also Boughts, then the situation is pretty straight-forward: Amazon doesn't know whom to recommend it to, so it just won't recommend it. Sounds horrible, right? Well, it's what happens whenever you launch a book. You first have to generate sales before Amazon can figure out what your Also Boughts are.

```
Note: Amazon is constantly experimenting with and A/B testing
Also Boughts. You won't find them on every product page, and
sometimes they'll be replaced by "Customers who read this book
also read ..." or "Customers who viewed this item also viewed
..." But if they don't show up on a product page, that doesn't
mean the book doesn't have any Also Boughts in the internal
Amazon system--that only happens when a book hasn't sold enough
copies.
```

Now let's see what happens if you have the wrong Also Boughts. Let's say you have a historical fiction book that (1) is selling well and (2) has a bunch of reviews. Its Also Boughts are in pristine shape: they're all related titles in your genre. However, you've been applying for a BookBub Featured Deal in Historical Fiction for ages, but keep getting turned down. So one day you try applying for BookBub's Historical Romance category instead, since your book has a bit of romance here and there. And surprise! You get accepted.

After the celebratory champagne, you spend your BookBub Deal day watching your book soar up the rankings. It hits number one in all its categories, so you go to bed happy. When you wake up, though, you notice that your Also Boughts are full of steamy historical romances. "Hmm, that's weird. But who cares? I'm number one!"

After a few days, your sales tank—and a month or two later, your book is barely selling a few copies a day. What happened? You messed up your Also Boughts.

See, when the AIRS detected that your book was selling well, it thought, "Hey, this book's a winner! Let's give it a push!" So it started e-mailing readers of the other books in your Also Boughts to give them a heads-up about your book.

Now, the AIRS is clever. It won't spam millions of readers without knowing for sure that they'll like your book. So it's going to *test* your book first. It'll start by recommending your book to a thousand readers or so, based on your Also Boughts. But guess what? *You've just messed up your Also Boughts.* These romance readers are going to check out your book, see that it's not 100 percent romance, and leave. The AIRS is going to think, "Huh, I guess it wasn't a winner after all," and stop recommending your book.

Getting out of a situation like this is *very* difficult. Cleaning up wrong Also Boughts generated by a BookBub deal (meaning thousands of sales) takes months. And if you think I'm exaggerating, I recommend you read David Gaughran's article "Amazon Recommendations and Also Boughts" on his blog.[21] This very thing happened to him.

What's the message in all this? You want to take great care of your Also Boughts. Make sure you only list your book in categories in which it 100 percent fits. Don't promote it to readers who aren't your target audience. Don't accept if an author in an unrelated genre offers to recommend it to their list. When it comes to Amazon, selling your book to the wrong people can be more detrimental in the long term than not selling it at all.

22

Amazon URL tips & tricks

Have you ever heard about authors who've had some of their reviews automatically taken down by Amazon without prior warning? It happens pretty regularly and is triggered when Amazon suspects that the reviews are *biased*, i.e., left by friends and relatives.

So how does Amazon identify such "friends and family reviews"? It looks at a number of things, but one of the main ones is the URL—the link—the reviewer used to access the book page and leave the review. In this chapter, I'll explain why, how to avoid getting street team reviews deleted, and more fun Amazon URL trivia.

Amazon's time-stamped search URLs

Say you want to share the Amazon link to one of your books. Maybe you're sending it to a friend. Naturally, you might:

1. Head to Amazon.com.
2. Enter your book title into the search bar.
3. Click on your book and land on its Amazon page.
4. Share the URL of that Amazon page with your friend.

To give you an example, I just did this with David Gaughran's excellent book

Let's Get Digital. I searched for "lets get digital" and clicked on the first result. I got the following URL: https://www.amazon.com/Lets-Get-Digital-Self-Publish-Publishing/dp/1983680354/ref=sr_1_1?ie=UTF8&qid=1532003911 &sr=8-1&keywords=lets+get+digital

As you can see, the full URL contains the keywords I searched for. But it also contains an important parameter: QID.

QID is a timestamp of when the search was made. It records the number of seconds that have passed since January 1, 1970. If I were to do the exact same search a second later, the QID in the URL would be *qid=1532003912*.

This means that every link you generate through an Amazon search is *unique*. Amazon knows when the search was made and what keyword it was related to. If its algorithms detect that a large percentage of a book's reviews come from readers who got to the book through the same time-stamped URL, they'll likely identify these reviews as biased and remove them.

For example, such a link was shared on Reddit by Trump supporters who wanted to "brigade" Megyn Kelly's book with one-star reviews. Because Amazon could identify all the reviews that came from that single link, they were able to delete them. (See the news story in the endnotes.[22])

So which link should you use instead? One that is stripped of any parameters—or everything that comes after the first long number. In the case of *Let's Get Digital*, it would be: https://www.amazon.com/Lets-Get-Digital-Self-Publish-Publishing/dp/1983680354/

You can even remove the part between *.com* and */dp/* and just have: https://www.amazon.com/dp/1983680354/

That's what we call a *clean link*, and the kind of link you can share safely with your friends, followers, and street team. You can also use affiliate links from the Amazon Associates Program, since those have no keyword tagging nor timestamps.

Will this be enough to *guarantee* you're safe from any review deletion? Probably not, since Amazon has other automated ways of flagging biased reviews. But it might reduce the risk a lot.

Turn your Amazon URLs into universal URLs

I'm guessing your readers aren't all in the US, are they? So if you send everyone to the Amazon.com store, those outside the US will first have to switch stores before they can buy your book.

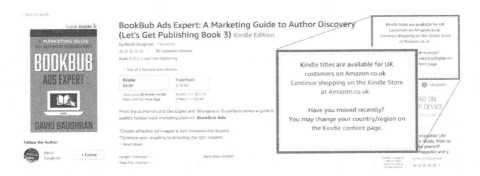

Wouldn't it be great if you could remove this step for them?

Well, you can: by sharing a *universal* Amazon URL. There are several tools you can use for that, but the two I generally recommend (because they're free) are Books2Read's Universal Links and Booklinker, both of which are included in the endnotes.[23]

Just paste a *clean* link to your book into either tool, and Books2Read or Booklinker will generate a link that will automatically send readers to their preferred country store.

Review page URLS

If the purpose of the link is to get people to review the book, there is a much better way to achieve this. By working some Amazon URL magic, you can generate a link that sends readers straight to any book's review page.

It's pretty simple magic, too. You need only copy and paste this URL: https://www.amazon.com/review/create-review?asin=ASIN and replace the letters "ASIN" with your book's ASIN, which you can find in the Product Details section. For example, the review page link for *Let's Get Digital* is:

https://www.amazon.com/review/create-review?asin=1983680354

Don't believe me? Here's the evidence:

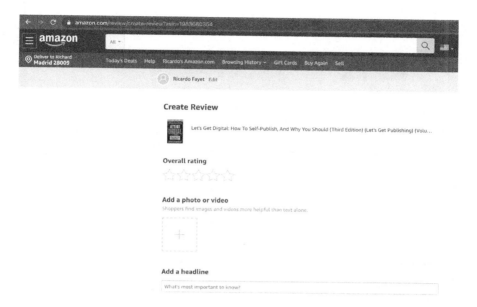

The series collection page

I already mentioned series collections in the section about series, but you might be wondering how to get such a page that lists all of your books in a given series. (Note: these are only available for Kindle books, not print.)

The Miracle Morning (14 book series)

Kindle Edition

From Book 1: "Hal Elrod is a genius and his book *The Miracle Morning* has been magical in my life. What Hal has done is taken the best practices, developed over centuries of human consciousness development, and condensed the 'best of the best' into a daily morning ritual. A ritual that is now part of my day."

| All Formats | Kindle Edition |

—**Robert Kiyosaki, bestselling author of** *Rich Dad Poor Dad*

What's being widely regarded as "one of the most life changing books ever written" may be the simplest approach to achieving everything you've ever

˅ Read more

☐ Hide books already in your library

1

The Miracle Morning: The Not-So-Obvious Secret Guaranteed to Transform Your Life (Before 8AM)
by Hal Elrod (Author) , Robert Kiyosaki (Foreword)
☆☆☆☆☆ (4,259)
Currently Unavailable
"Hal Elrod is a genius and his book *The Miracle Morning* has been magical in my life. What Hal has done is taken the best practices, developed over centuries of human consciousness development, and condensed the 'best of
˅ Read more

Other Formats: Audible Audiobook , Hardcover , Paperback

2

The Miracle Morning for Real Estate Agents: It's Your Time to Rise and Shine

The series collection page for the Miracle Morning books

When you upload your book to Amazon via KDP, you can enter a series title and a series volume number. If you use *the exact same* title and the right volume numbers, Amazon *should* create that series page automatically.

If they don't, you used to have to reach out manually to KDP Support to ask them to set it up for you. Thankfully, as of November 2020, that's not the case anymore: you can now create series pages directly within your KDP dashboard. Just click on "Create and manage a series," add all the ASINs you want to include in the series, and ta-da! KDP even offers you the possibility to write a custom description for the series page — if you don't, they'll just pull up the description of book one.

The multi "Add to Cart" link

This is one I'm borrowing from Joe Konrath (one of the first voices of self-publishing) and Mark Dawson (who alerted me about it)—and it has to do with multiauthor promos on Amazon.

See, Joe ran a free promotion with several other indie authors who all discounted their respective books to free. Nothing new and groundbreaking so far. But here's the cool thing: he created a super Amazon URL that *automatically added all these books to readers' carts*. Genius, right?

So what does this URL look like? It's pretty simple, really. I'm going to shorten it and deconstruct it for you: https://www.amazon.com/gp/aws/-cart/add.html?AssociateTag=reedwebs-20&ASIN.1=B07SVHCJT2&Quan-tity.1=1&ASIN.2=B017G610AY&Quantity.2=1&[...]&add=ADD+ALL+TO+AMA-ZON+US+CART.

- The first bit is just the standard "Add to Cart" Amazon URL: *https://www.amazon.com/gp/aws/cart/add.html.*
- Then comes the associate tag, which you can remove if you don't have an Amazon Associates account.
- And then come the ASINs and quantities of all the books to add to the cart. The quantity is always "1": *ASIN.1=B07SVHCJT2&Quantity.1=1.*
- Finally, the last self-explanatory bit tells Amazon to add all of it to the cart: *add=ADD+ALL+TO+AMAZON+US+CART.*

Setting up such a URL manually can admittedly be a bit tiring, which is why I created a whole spreadsheet for it. You'll find the link to it in the endnotes,[24] as well as a guide for using it.

23

Kindle Unlimited vs. wide

I've made reference to Kindle Unlimited several times in this section, so it's only fitting that I close it with a deep dive into what Kindle Unlimited is, how it impacts visibility on the Kindle Store, and whether you should opt in to it ... at the price of exclusivity.

The pros of Amazon exclusivity

If you've already published an e-book through KDP, you know that Amazon offers you the option of being *exclusive* to them through a program called KDP Select. This practically means that you cannot give away or sell your e-book *on any other platform*—and that you lose potential sales on Apple, Barnes & Noble, Kobo, and so on.

In exchange for your exclusivity, Amazon offers a series of advantages. You can read about them on the KDP Select landing page, but the most important incentive, by far, is the inclusion in Kindle Unlimited (KU).

KU has become so popular among Amazon readers that in certain genres, a majority of them are subscribers. This makes it nearly impossible for non-KU authors to appeal to them, considering these readers can get a comparable book for free.

KU also has its own best seller charts and lists, and therefore its own ranking algorithms and automated recommendation systems. In other words, KU has its own ecosystem and requires a different form of marketing. Whether or not you want to be in KU, you need to understand *how that ecosystem works* because you're going to be impacted by it, either positively or negatively.

How does Kindle Unlimited work for an author?

Every month Amazon announces the size of the previous month's Kindle Direct Publishing Global Fund. This is the pot of money from which authors whose titles are available through Kindle Unlimited get paid. In April 2020, the total amount distributed by Amazon to KU authors and publishers was $30.3 million.

How does Amazon determine how to distribute this money across all the authors and publishers taking part in the program? It uses a simple metric: the number of pages read. In April 2020, a KU author would get paid $0.0042 per every page read. This amount varies slightly every month, but you can keep an eye on the variations thanks to a helpful post by Written Word Media.[25]

Given that a standard-length novel is generally between 300 and 400 pages, this means that KU authors get paid around $1.38–$1.84 for every reader who borrows and reads one of their books through to the end (we'll call that a *full borrow*). Note that the actual retail price of the book doesn't factor in these calculations. Whether you list your book at $0.99, $5.99, or $14.99, you'll get paid the same amount for every full borrow.

Now that you know how royalties work on Kindle Unlimited, it's time to look into how to make your book discoverable in the KU ecosystem.

How do book recommendations work for KU readers?

In many ways the system is similar to Amazon's overall recommendation system for Kindle eBooks. It relies on the usual two factors: sales and Also Boughts.

The main difference is that Amazon sends special recommendation e-mails to KU readers that only include KU books. These are the e-mails you want your KU book to be featured in. And these recommendations are powered mostly by Amazon's Popularity list.

What does this effectively mean? First, there's no virtuous circle on KU: while sales on Amazon automatically generate more sales (because your book climbs in the Pop list rankings, and the Pop list powers recommendations), more page reads won't magically generate more page reads (because page reads don't count on the Popularity list).

So you still need to market your book to non-KU readers. But the good news is, there's a very easy way to do it: running a free promotion. If you make your book free for five days and advertise it enough to generate a healthy number of downloads (shoot for at least five thousand), you should see a bump in page reads a few days later. Why? Because free downloads count (albeit a lot less than a sale, and with a four-day lag) on the Popularity list.

Again, there is a whole section in this book dedicated to price promotions, so I won't go into more detail for now.

So what does it take to succeed in KU?

If you want to be successful in KU, you'll need to (1) discount your books often (and keep that discounted price for longer than average), and (2) *heavily advertise* your price promotions through Facebook, Amazon, and BookBub ads.

Here's an example taken from David Gaughran's (yes, him again) excellent post on KU visibility:[26]

> *"Let's say you are launching Book 4 in a KU-enrolled series, and are wondering how to build a decent launch. A good approach might be to make Book 1 free for 5 days, and run a concurrent 99¢ Countdown deal on Book 2, and a $1.99 Countdown on Book 3. Maybe load all the ads on sites like ENT and Robin Reads on that free Book 1 and then give the whole series a push with a carousel ad on Facebook."*

Wait a second, all this is great—but aren't I losing a bunch of sales income by doing that? Yes, you are. But that's one of the principles of being in KU: you shouldn't be afraid to sacrifice sales to generate more page reads. That's where the real money is for you—so forget about immediate income. Focus on climbing the Popularity list and you should see a huge wave of page reads coming in (almost magically) three to four days after you end your promotion.

Now that you know what it takes to be successful in KU, let's start answering the million-dollar question: should you, or should you not, enroll your book(s) in Kindle Unlimited?

To KU or not to KU?

First consider your genre. As I mentioned, it's nearly impossible in some genres to sell well on Amazon if you're not in KU. And if you can't sell well on Amazon? Well, that makes it much, much harder to make a living off your writing.

Analyzing your categories

So how do you know whether you're in a KU-heavy genre? Just take a look at the best seller charts for your main category. You can access these charts through the "Bestsellers & More" tab on the Kindle Store. From there, select the main category you'd place your book in, and look at the proportion of KU titles in the top twenty or top fifty sellers.

For example, at the time of this writing:

- In the Science Fiction Best Seller list, seventeen of the top twenty titles are in KU.
- In the Fantasy Best Seller list, sixteen of the top twenty titles are in KU.
- In the Thriller Best Seller list, seven of the top twenty titles are in KU.
- In the Historical Fiction Best Seller list, eight of the top twenty titles are in KU.

- In the Self-Help Best Seller list, thirteen of the top twenty titles are in KU.

What does this mean? That Science Fiction and Fantasy are particularly KU-heavy genres right now. If you're writing in those genres, it's probably in your best interest to be exclusive to Amazon for your books.

Note: you can carry the same analysis through subcategories for niche genres like Urban Fantasy, Paranormal Romance, etc.

Series vs. standalones

Another thing to consider regardless of whether you're a fiction or nonfiction author is whether you're writing a series or a standalone book. As illustrated by David Gaughran's example above, the most effective promotion that can help you climb up the Popularity list involves discounting *several* books across a series—and then advertising the whole thing.

Also, one of the main goals of KU authors is to *hook* readers into their series or universe. Once a KU reader finishes a book in your series, it doesn't cost them anything to get the next one and keep reading. There's zero friction. So the longer your series (and the more you can hook readers into it), the more one customer will be worth to you.

How you feel about Amazon

Finally, a self-evident factor is how *you* feel about Amazon. Specifically, how do you feel about having all your eggs in their basket? Sure, KDP Select is only a ninety-day, renewable contract, but as we'll cover later in this book, building a presence outside of Amazon (e.g., on Apple Books, Kobo, Barnes & Noble, Google Play, etc.) takes *a lot* of time. If KU suddenly changes their rules and stops working for you, you'll be at a huge disadvantage when competing with long-established authors on other retailers.

I know many authors in KU-heavy genres who have resisted the KU appeal so far because of that very reason. Trusting one retailer with 100 percent of your income, whatever your business, is an incredibly risky thing to do. But Amazon is so good at making it worth your while—at least for now—that, well, it's a tough decision.

I hope this breakdown has helped you better understand KU and what it takes to be successful there. Of course, to make a fully informed decision about Amazon exclusivity, you should also have a good understanding of what you're leaving on the table when signing with KDP Select. In other words, you need to know what the other stores—Apple, Google Play, Kobo, and so on—have to offer. Which is exactly what the next section of this book is all about.

V

Wide marketing

A lot of information exists about Amazon marketing and visibility—but there's extremely little about Apple Books, Kobo, Google Play, Barnes & Noble, and other retailers. And yet I know many authors who make most of their living from "wide" retailer sales.
In this section you'll find exclusive tips to grow your sales on non-Amazon retailers, as well as an in-depth analysis of how the main ones work.

24

Selling on non-Amazon retailers

Before diving into each of the main non-Amazon retailers, I'm going to explore the philosophy and core principles around "going wide"—i.e., selling your books on more retailers than just Amazon.

The pros of selling wide

A big reason "wide authors" choose to opt out of Amazon exclusivity is simple: they want to make their books available in as many places as possible. It's a simple marketing principle: the more stores where your product is available, the more you're likely to sell. But the problem nowadays is that you have to choose between wide stores ... and Kindle Unlimited. You just can't be *everywhere*, and your choice ultimately boils down to "KU vs. wide." By doing some market research, you should be able to figure out how KU-heavy your genre is (i.e., an estimated market share of Kindle Unlimited in your genre), and make your decision based on that.

More importantly, Amazon may represent 80 percent of the global e-book market, but it's also the most competitive store, the one where visibility costs the most—both figuratively and literally, since Amazon Advertising came out. So while non-Amazon retailers are much smaller, they're somewhat easier to get a foothold on.

Finally, the main reason many authors opt for a wide distribution strategy is because of, well, Amazon. They don't want to put all their eggs in just one basket, especially one they have no control over whatsoever. Kindle Unlimited was a boon to many authors when it came out, but it also hurt many more. The same will happen every time Amazon changes its rules or its algorithms, or releases a new service. The more income streams you have, the less dependent you'll be on the retail giant.

Note: If you want to be totally independent from retailers, you also have the option of selling directly from your website. This is not something I cover in this book, as I believe it only really makes sense for specific formats (e.g. special edition hardbacks), but if you want to learn more about it, I recommend reading Joanna Penn's blog post on the topic[27].

Going wide: A long-term strategy

The first thing to say about going wide is that it's not a quick-buck strategy. It's not like Kindle Unlimited, where you can run price promos, blast your books with the famous advertising cocktail (Amazon ads, Facebook ads, BookBub ads), and see instant results.

I know several authors who make as much money (or more) outside Amazon, but they all have one thing in common: they've been committed to "being wide" from the start.

Building a presence and garnering sales on Apple Books, Barnes & Noble, Kobo, or Google Play *takes time*. It also takes a different marketing approach (slower, more long-term). So if you're not seeing any sales on these retailers in the months following your book launch, don't panic and rush into Amazon exclusivity. In most cases, it will take more than a year to see decent sales outside of the retail giant.

How to distribute to non-Amazon retailers

To distribute your e-book to Kobo, Apple Books, Barnes & Noble, or Google Play, you have two options:

- "Go direct" by using each store's own proprietary e-book publishing platform.
- Use an aggregator to reach all of them at once.

If you're not familiar with e-book publishing platforms and aggregators, you'll find everything you need to know in Reedsy's e-book distribution guide. (See the link in the endnotes.[28]) I personally recommend using Draft2Digital to avoid the hassle of logging in to *every single* publishing platform each time you want to publish a new book, update your metadata, or run a price promotion.

The downside to using an aggregator is that you'll lose some perks (on top of paying them a small percentage of your royalties). I'll highlight those perks over the next few chapters as we explore each main retailer in more depth.

Discoverability outside Amazon

There's one huge difference between Amazon and the rest of the retailers when it comes to discoverability. While everything on Amazon is run by *algorithms*, the best visibility spots on Apple Books, Kobo, and Barnes & Noble are *curated by humans*. Only Google Play could be considered as predominantly *algorithmic*, and even the best visibility spots there are hand-curated.

I insist a lot on "algorithmic" vs. "human" curation in the next few chapters, so let me give you some concrete examples of both right away.

If you have an Apple device and open your Apple Books app, you'll see something like this:

Apple Books home page on desktop app

See the carousel of banners at the top? These all link to collections of books that have been put together by the Apple Books merchandising team. As such, they're a prime example of *human* curation: it's a human being (or a team of human beings) who decide which books get included in those collections.

If you look at the section immediately below the banner carousel, it's called "Bestsellers." Almost all stores will have a section for best sellers, which they'll generally feature quite prominently. That list is a perfect example of *algorithmic* curation: it's simply a list of books that have sold the most copies over the past few days. It's not decided by a human, but by a simple sales algorithm.

What does this mean? Well, selling more on non-Amazon retailers requires a much more *human* approach.

Building connections with company reps

One of the most effective ways to get into special features and promos on these stores is to build a connection with someone from the company.

That's where writers' conferences can come in handy. You'll find Kobo, Barnes & Noble, and sometimes Apple reps at most big writing conferences (think Romance Writers of America, Novelists, Inc., ThrillerFest, etc.). Go talk to them. Now, don't stalk them and sneak your book into their bags when they're not looking. Instead, offer to buy them a drink (surprise: book people like to drink!), ask them for tips to get more sales on their platform, and tweet or retweet them during panels.

Sending your readers to non-Amazon retailers

Making friends with reps isn't a requirement, though, and it certainly isn't enough to get features or promos on their stores. Merchandising teams all share the same goal: *to drive more sales.* So you've got to prove to them that your books can sell on their store.

How do you do that? Well, you actively promote your book specifically on these retailers and start generating some sales on your own. For example:

- Include link buttons to your book on Apple Books, Kobo, Barnes & Noble, etc. on your website.
- Set up preorders exclusive to Apple Books and Kobo. (I'll tell you why in a later chapter.)
- Do cover reveals and exclusive sneak peeks on Apple Books.
- Run Facebook ads targeted at interests like "Apple Books," "Kobo e-readers," etc. (crossed with your usual interests), and promote your book's page on these retailers.
- Run price promotions and use promotion sites with a known non-Amazon readership (e.g., BookBub and Bargain Booksy).

The great news is that wide books have a much higher chance of being accepted for a BookBub Featured Deal than KU books. (Don't worry, this book has a whole section about BookBub.)

A single Featured Deal will skyrocket your sales on *all retailers*, which will likely get the attention of the merchandising teams, who may in turn feature your book in their promos, driving even more sales ... and *that's* how you build a presence on non-Amazon retailers.

In the next few chapters, we take a more in-depth look at three of the main wide retailers: Apple Books, Google Play, and Kobo. "What about Barnes & Noble?" you may ask. Well, at this point (the end of 2020), the future of B&N is very much uncertain. Also, it's a similar store to Apple Books, and one you can easily decipher once you know how to analyze it. So for the sake of avoiding repetition, I haven't included it in this book.

25

Apple Books

When it comes to selling e-books, many view Apple Books as Amazon's main competitor. And that hunch is backed up by the numbers. A 2015 analysis by the (now defunct) Author Earnings website showed that Apple Books' market share in the US was bigger than that of Barnes & Noble, Kobo, and Google Play combined.

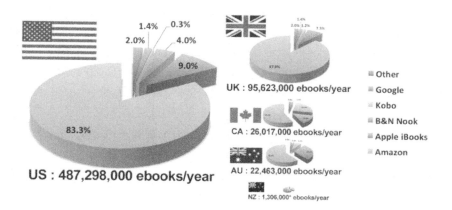

Source: Author Earnings

It's still under 10 percent of the total US e-book market, which feels small when compared to Amazon's more than 80 percent. But with the rise of

Kindle Unlimited, which has lured many authors into Amazon exclusivity, it may be easier for authors to get a big chunk of Apple's 10 percent than a small chunk of Amazon's 83 percent.

That is, if you play your cards right. And that's exactly what I'll show you how to do in this chapter.

A different kind of readership

While there's no official statistic to confirm this, it's common knowledge that Apple Books readers are less sensitive to price. After all, most Apple Books readers own Apple devices, and those aren't exactly cheap. Essentially, this means that you can get traction for a five dollar or six dollar book more easily on Apple than on Amazon.

Even better, Apple is one of the *only* retailers who don't price match. So while it's not super fair to their readers, you can try pricing your book *a bit* higher on Apple Books than you do on Amazon, Google Play, Kobo, or Barnes & Noble.

Where Apple Books readers' tolerance of higher prices pays off, though, is on mega box sets (don't worry, there's a chapter all about box sets at the end of this book). You probably know that Amazon pays you only 35 percent in royalties on books priced above $9.99. Well, Apple doesn't have that upper limit: you still earn 70 percent in royalties on sales at $10.99, $19.99, or even $24.99. And Apple customers won't be scared by these price points. This makes Apple Books a perfect place to sell exclusive box sets.

You might not sell a lot of them, but each sale will be worth a good dinner. More importantly, the Apple Books team tends to reward *exclusivity* a lot: if they see that your box set is only available on Apple and is doing well, they'll be all the more tempted to give it more visibility on the store.

A preorder paradise

Perhaps the best advantage of Apple Books when compared to Amazon is this secret weapon: preorders. If you get a preorder sale on Amazon, it counts (toward Best Seller list rankings and Popularity lists) as one sale at the time of the preorder. On Apple Books it counts as one sale at the time of the preorder—and then as another sale on launch day.

This means that if you manage to get five hundred preorders on Apple Books, your book will shoot to the top of the ranks on launch day (and attract the attention of the merchandising team). Some authors take advantage of this by offering *Apple Books–exclusive* preorders, meaning their readers are only able to preorder the books on Apple. This might lose them some preorder sales on other retailers, but in turn makes the Apple merchandising team very happy. And a happy merch team generally equates to more visibility for your books, especially on a store as *human-curated* as Apple Books.

A store curated by human beings

As we saw in the introductory chapter to this wide marketing section, the top visibility spots on the Apple Books store home page are reserved for *human-curated* sections, like the banner carousel at the top.

And that's the main feature of the Apple Store that sets it apart from Amazon or Google Play: visibility very much depends on *human curation* rather than algorithms. So your ultimate goal on Apple Books should be to catch the attention of their merchandising team—they'll unlock a whole new world of possibilities. Of course, to do so, you'll first need to sell a bit on your own, which is what the rest of the tips in this chapter are for.

You'll also find several sections below that top banner. For example:

- **Bestsellers:** similar to the Top Charts (see below), but with a slightly different algorithm
- **Read It Before You Watch It:** books that have been adapted to film or television
- **New This Week**: new releases of the past week
- **Limited Time: Under $4:** a selection of discounted books manually curated by the Apple Books merchandising team
- **Coming Soon:** books on preorder
- **First in a Series: Free:** also manually curated by the Apple Books merchandising team

Apple Books charts and rankings

What's *not* so different from other stores is that best-selling books still get the lion's share of visibility. The Bestsellers section is often the first on the main Featured page, and the next two tabs in the top navigation are also all about sales:

- **Top Charts:** similar to Amazon, the Top Charts are split into Paid and Free, and rank the books by number of recent sales
- **The New York Times**: the books in this week's *NYT* fiction and nonfiction best seller lists

Categories and subcategories

More interesting is how the store handles categories. If you're a reader looking for books in a specific category, you have to use a somewhat hidden drop-down menu in the right sidebar of the home page, or go to the Categories tab in the top navigation bar.

The Categories menu will only list broad, top-level categories like Mysteries & Thrillers or Sci-Fi & Fantasy. If you select one, you can then view collections that allow you to drill down into more niche genres:

Some of these collections will bring you to what is essentially a subcategory page with similar sections to those on the home page: Bestsellers, New

Releases, Free Series Starters, and so on.

Other collections, though, are manually curated selections of books that meet certain criteria. That's the case for the First in a Series Science Fiction collection and the Science Fiction Essentials collection.

Again, this goes to show the importance of manual curation, as well as the prominence of free series starters, which are featured nearly everywhere on commercial fiction genre pages.

Some top-level categories, like History, don't feature collections for subgenres. Instead, they have dedicated sections:

I believe the books in those sections are manually selected, but they might also be automatically curated based on the subcategories selected during the upload process.

Of course, if readers are searching for books in a specific niche genre or topic, they probably won't use the Categories list—they'll just use the search bar. Which is why it's just as important to look at how search works on the Apple Books store.

Keyword matches in the title, subtitle, and author name

The best way to explore this is simply to run a few searches and analyze what results are presented to the reader. Let's start with a nonfiction example.

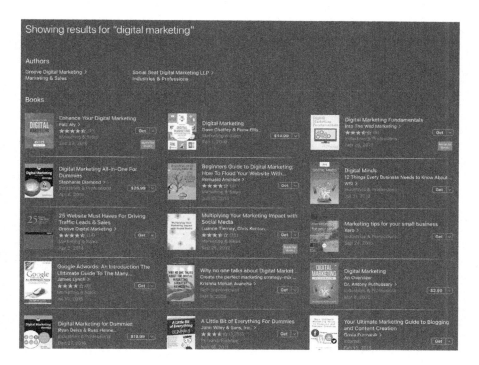

What immediately strikes me is that *all* of the top five books in this search have the phrase "digital marketing" in the title. The sixth one, *Digital Minds*, has that exact keyword phrase in its subtitle. And the seventh one has it in its author name.

What this tells me is that having a keyword present in your title, subtitle, or author name probably increases your likelihood of ranking for that keyword. But that's just a hypothesis for now. Let's look at other searches to validate it.

When I search for "dragon fantasy," all of the top fifteen books have the word "dragon" in the title. But they don't have the phrase "dragon fantasy," which tells me that:

1. Keyword match in the title is indeed an important ranking factor.
2. Apple is able to understand that searches for "dragon fantasy" are searches for "dragon" in books listed in at least one fantasy category.

Here's a final case study:

Again, most of the books have a variant of "cozy witch mysteries" in either the title, series title, or subtitle. There's only one that doesn't (*Catatonic*)—but we'll get into the reason later.

What I'm interested in here is this: why is *Cozy Witch Mysteries* ranked number one for that search? It has no reviews, so it probably doesn't sell well compared to the others below it. And it was published in 2017, so it has no recency. That leaves one reason in my eyes: it has an exact keyword match with the search.

To validate that assumption, let's run a similar (but slightly different) search:

As you can see, most of the results here, while they overlap a little with the first search, are different—as are the rankings. Most importantly, the first two books in this example have "witch cozy mystery" in their titles—which validates our assumption that an exact (or almost exact) match in the title is rewarded above all else on the Apple Books store.

Keyword matches in the book description

Now let's get back to that *Catatonic* book that was ranking for the "cozy witch mysteries" search—without having "witch," "cozy," *or* "mystery" in the title, subtitle, or series title! How come it's even showing up in that search?

Well, because all of those words are in the book description. Let's look at another example:

Most of the books here have "Victorian" in their title, series title, and/or subtitle, except for *The Mesmerist*. If we click on that book and read its description, we find: *"The Mesmerist is the first in a five-book multiauthor Victorian romance time travel series."* (Emphasis mine.)

And if we search for "time travel series," we'll also find this book—albeit in the forty-second position. So while it isn't as powerful as an exact match in your title, having the keyword in your blurb *does* play a role in the Apple Book store's search algorithm.

Sales and downloads

"Wait! If it's more important to have the keyword in the title than in the description, how come The Mesmerist *in your example is ranking* above *several books that have 'Victorian romance' in their titles?"*

Excellent question! This allows me to nicely transition to the last important factor in the Apple Books search algorithm: sales and downloads.

Now, Apple Books doesn't show the rank of the book on the product page, like Amazon does—so we have no way of telling whether one book sells more than another. We can try to guess that through reviews, but that's about it.

We can see that *The Mesmerist* has quite a few reviews. More importantly, the fact that it's a five-book series tells me that it's probably getting a lot of promo. Which means that it's selling well—better than the books below it in the search.

Let's look at a much broader search to validate this assumption:

Here, most of the books have the word "thriller" in the titles. The only exceptions are the two household names, which are probably selling like hotcakes right now. This goes to show that sales are, indeed, an important factor in Apple search rankings. Even if you don't have a keyword match in your titles, you can still rank highly for that keyword—*if* you get a lot of sales.

But it's not *just* sales. Seven out of the top twelve results for "thriller" are *free* books. Which tells me that Apple Books' search algorithm probably gives somewhat similar weight to a free download as it does to a sale.

This is in stark contrast to Amazon, which has a search algorithm that privileges higher-priced sales and weights free downloads at 1/100th of a sale (more or less). Search for "thriller" on the Kindle Store, and I guarantee that none of the books you'll find on the first few pages will be free.

That's it for my analysis of the Apple Books store! You'll notice that I haven't made specific recommendations. I'm not telling you, for example, to stuff your title and book description with keywords (that's bad practice and Apple Books won't allow it). My aim is just to show you how readers (probably) find books on the store. Now it's up to you to leverage that knowledge to increase your books' discoverability!

26

Google Play

Google Play is probably the least popular retailer among indie authors, despite the huge reach of the Google brand and their Google Play store. The reason is because until mid-2019, it was *incredibly difficult* to distribute to Google Play. You couldn't reach them via the most popular aggregators (Draft2Digital and Smashwords), and while they had an online platform to upload and distribute a book directly to their store, that platform was invite only.

Worse, if you managed to get in and sell your book on Google Play, the store would often automatically discount it without prior warning, which would trigger price matching from Amazon and generally mess up your whole marketing plan.

For all these reasons, I used to recommend that authors skip Google Play altogether. *Now*, though, this has changed. Not only has Google Play gotten rid of most of these drawbacks, they seem to be investing more resources into their Books section—a welcome sight in times when Amazon's dominance seems ineluctable.

All in all, this means that—unless you're exclusive to Amazon through KDP Select—there is no reason anymore not to have your books on Google Play. On the contrary, you have everything to gain.

Of course, uploading your book to the Google Play store is the easy bit. Getting it to sell—that's another story. But that's what this whole chapter focuses on.

A store unique to each reader

The first step to boost your sales on *any* retailer is to understand how readers search for and buy books on it. So if you have an Android device, open your Google Play app, go to the Books section, and take a look at how it's structured.

If you're on desktop, just go to play.google.com/books, and then click on "Shop" in the sidebar. That'll bring you to the Google Play Books home page, which is probably the entry point for *all* readers when they're searching for their next read.

Now, the biggest particularity of the Google Play Books store home page is that it is *unique* to each reader. In the words of the Google Play Books team:

Nearly all of Google Play Books' merchandising is driven by an algorithm. As a result, every reader sees a different personalized bookstore. If books are removed from the store, it disrupts the algorithm's learning about those titles and eliminates the opportunity for those titles to be recommended. More time in the store and more lifetime sales translate to higher discoverability.

Now, this learning process and customization is not unique to Google. Amazon does it as well through Also Boughts, and on its Kindle eBooks home page, which is also customized for each reader.

But here's the big difference: *most Amazon readers never see that Kindle eBooks home page*. It takes several hard-to-find clicks to access that page from the main Amazon home page. On Google Play, it takes one click—so the home page is all the more important.

A focus on deals

Every time I visit the Google Play Books store, the home page seems to give *a lot* of visibility to deals, i.e., free, cheap, or temporarily discounted books:

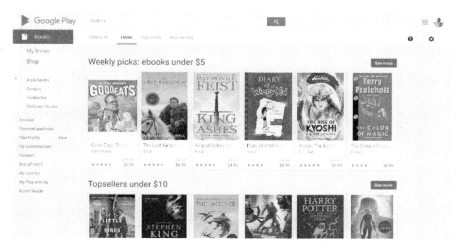

Combine that with the fact that you can schedule price promos in advance within the Google Play Books Partner Center, and that tells you how important discounts and promos are for visibility on the store.

> Pro tip: If you're going to run a price promotion on Google
> Play, make sure to do so via the Promotions section of the
> Partner Center. If you take advantage of that--instead of just
> manually lowering a book's list price in the metadata--it will
> trigger a strikethrough of your title's list prices in the store.

Free series starters

Speaking of sections that tend to be prominently featured on home pages, here's a particularly interesting one:

Free scifi & fantasy series starters

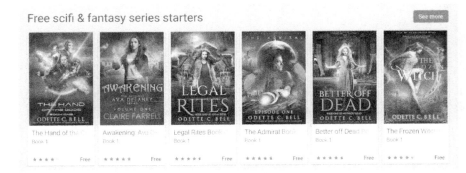

Of course, it's only relevant to series authors, but in case you didn't get the message in this book already: *you should be writing in series!* Google Play has several sections throughout the store dedicated to series, and in particular "free first-in-series." It's something they have in common with Amazon, and a great opportunity for all wide series authors—as long as you're OK making book one free.

But don't take it from me! Here's a quote from Charlotte Byrd, an indie author who's done particularly well on the Google Play store:

> *"The one thing I recently did that I have never done before was make three of my first-in-series free. I got a BookBub Featured Deal, which I had never gotten before, and I decided to make two other series starters free along with it during this difficult time. I have seen my sales increase significantly as a result (not just as a result of the BookBub, but even before that promotion went through). I have very strong read through, and with having the first book free, I am seeing a number of my books in the catalog appear on Google Play charts and stay there. That's another thing I really like about Google Play: the books have a lot more stickability on the charts than on other platforms.*
>
> *Also, I wrote [to my Google Play rep] and told her about my free series starters. She placed that into a special feature section, and I'm seeing a lot of read through from that.*
>
> *I always run Facebook ads with a good-sized budget to support my first-in-series, and now I'm finding that the ads are a lot more efficient*

and a lot cheaper because they are promoting a free book. I am sending the ads to my website where readers who use Google Play can get the book."

What can we learn from this? First, free series starters work really well on Google Play. But also, all these Free [Genre] Series Starters sections throughout the store are *human-curated* sections. Your book will only be featured there if someone from the Google Play merchandising team includes it.

Finally, this example also goes to show that free downloads count toward the Google Play charts and algorithms—granting them a lot more visibility than on Amazon (where free books are on a separate list).

New arrivals

If you look at the top of the Google Play store home page, one of the main navigation elements you'll see is New Arrivals. This gives new releases a great deal of visibility on the store. From some quick research, I found that new books seemingly feature on this page during their first thirty days—making this section similar to Amazon's Hot New Releases, except it gets extra visibility.

This makes rapid-releasing an attractive option, as it allows you to get several titles with similar branding in the list—with the goal of catching the eyes of readers.

All good stuff so far, right? But the *most interesting* bit about the Google Play store—and where the biggest opportunities lie for you—is in its search algorithm.

The search algorithm

Unlike Google's search algorithm—the most sophisticated one on the web—Google Play's search algorithm looks a little bit ... basic. And that means you can get your book to rank for the searches you want if you're clever about it. So where do you start?

Based on my own (experimental) research, it looks like Google places much more importance on keyword matches in the title and/or subtitle, categories, and blurb than Amazon. Inversely, it seems to place less importance on *sales*. Which means you can get your book to rank highly for competitive searches—even if it's not selling well yet!

Let's look at a few examples.

Keyword match in title

When I search for "dragon romance," all the books that Google Play returns have "dragon" in the title. When I click on "See more" in the top right, I discover that *forty-nine of the top fifty books* ranking for this term also have "dragon" in either the title or series title.

The only one that doesn't have the keyword "dragon" in its title includes it several times in the blurb.

Keyword match in blurb

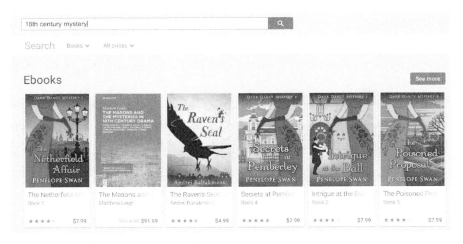

Now, this search is particularly interesting in that:

1. The one book with a keyword match is a *nonfiction* book (which is probably not the searcher's intent, but it's still showing up prominently).
2. All the other books don't have that keyword anywhere else but in their
blurbs.

What does this mean? Google Play indexes *whole book descriptions* and uses
them to rank books in searches. Sadly, a lot of authors have already figured
this out. As a result, we're seeing a lot of keyword dumping in blurbs.

I don't believe the store will allow keyword dumping for long, since the
Google Play team is aware of it. So I definitely don't recommend it, but
it goes to show that keywords *matter* in blurbs, so you should try to work
relevant ones *naturally* into your book description.

Here's another example, from a search for "espionage thriller:"

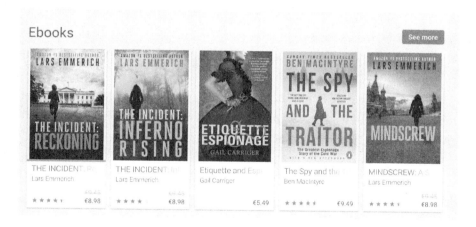

In this case, most of the books in the results have "espionage" or "spy"
in the title, subtitle, or blurb. If you click on "See more," however, you'll
see a lot more results that don't necessarily have "espionage" (or a related
keyword) in the blurb. What they all *do* have in common is that they're in
the Fiction / Thrillers / Espionage genre category. Which leads me to my
next point.

Keyword match in category

When publishing your book on Google Play, you can select *as many categories as you want* using BISAC codes. But when it comes to browsing the store, you'll see that all BISAC subcategories are not available.

So what does Google Play do with all the categories you feed in? Well, they use them for the search algorithm. If you search for "espionage" books, you'll find that almost all the results have selected "espionage thriller" as one of their categories.

It's less powerful than a keyword match in your title, but probably as powerful as—if not more than—a keyword match in the blurb (again, based on my anecdotal research). So make sure to choose your categories wisely!

Phrase matches and search intent

Now, all this makes the search algorithm seem pretty simplistic. It's not, but it does have some flaws. Let's analyze a search for "martial arts," for example.

The search mostly returns books that are 100 percent relevant ... except for one: *The Art of War*. It's a great book, and most of what you'll learn in it applies to martial arts, but ... it's not a book on martial arts.

So why is it there? Because Google Play uses *semantic search*—meaning it seeks to group keywords by topic. And it probably identified "martial" to be close enough to "war" to understand "martial arts" as "war arts," hence the Sun Tzu result.

Here's another example that's much more blatant:

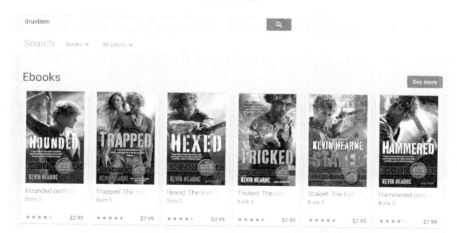

If you search for "druidism" on Amazon, you'll get books on druidism and other earth-based religions. But here on Google Play, you're pointed to a *fiction* series—just because the word "druid" is in the series title.

All in all, it seems that the Google Play search algorithm still has a long way to go to properly understand readers' search intent. This, however, provides you with some huge opportunities if you understand how it works.

27

Kobo

So far, we've seen two stores that are very different in essence (Apple Books with human curation vs. Google Play with an algorithmic approach) that still have a lot of things in common: prominent hand-curated sections for free series starters, an emphasis on "free" in general with free downloads counting toward search rank algorithms, and a clear preference for series in commercial fiction genres.

With this in mind, I'll do a third and last store analysis for Kobo. Why Kobo and not Barnes & Noble? First, as I mentioned a few chapters ago, the future of B&N is uncertain. More importantly, Kobo has been growing its market share quite a bit in non-US territories and has a unique model worth looking into.

That said, this whole section on non-Amazon retailers is as much here to give you practical tips for success on "wide stores," as it is to show you how to *replicate* this analysis for any other store you're interested in. This is particularly important because retailers change rapidly, and I can't promise I'll keep updating this book every time they do! So make sure you run this analysis every once in a while to detect changes that would require you to change your strategy.

I'll give you an example: say that Apple Books changes their search algorithm to lower the importance of exact matches in title or subtitle, and increase the importance of sales. If you detect that, you might want to rename your books or change your strategy to keep your rankings.

With that out of the door, let's dive into Kobo.

More than a retailer: A global distributor

The first thing you should know about Kobo is that it's not just a retailer. While Apple Books and Google Play Books are global *online stores* for e-books, Kobo is more. Of course, Kobo has a store (kobo.com) where it sells e-books and audiobooks in dozens of different countries and territories. That store is similar to any other online retailer, and it's what I'll mostly analyze in this chapter.

But here's the additional thing: when you distribute a book through Kobo (whether you do it through Kobo Writing Life or an aggregator like Draft2Digital), your book will not just be made available on the Kobo.com store. It'll *also* be distributed by Kobo to hundreds of local retailers and libraries[29]—like Fnac in France, Mondadori in Italy, or Walmart.

How much can you expect to sell on these local partner stores? Not much, since they're all pretty small. (I mean, Walmart is *big* in general—but it's small in the e-book world.) That said, the compound effect of all these local stores might turn into a regular trickle of income for you, which is always nice to have!

In any case, from now on I'm going to concentrate on where the vast majority of your Kobo sales will come from: the Kobo.com store.

Global, yes, but Canadian first

When analyzing how visibility works on Apple Books and Google Play, I naturally looked at their US stores—because those comprise their biggest market by far.

With Kobo, it's different: the US is most definitely *not* their biggest market. In fact, according to data from former Director of Self-Publishing & Author Relations, Mark Leslie Lefebvre,[30] the US was only the fourth biggest market for Kobo in 2017, behind Canada, the United Kingdom, and Australia.

While this has probably changed in the past three years, you can still expect the majority of your Kobo sales to come from their Canadian store. In fact, when running Facebook ads for authors recently, I found that ads pointing to their Canadian store (targeting a Canadian audience) converted *a lot* better than US ads pointing to their Walmart store.

For the rest of this analysis, I'll focus on the Canadian store. You can find it pretty easily: just go to kobo.com and click on the flag in the top bar. Next, select "Canada." (It'll be first in the list—another sign that it's Kobo's biggest market.)

Human curation and power to audio

Now, the first things that stand out to me about the home page are that:

1. They're pushing audiobooks pretty hard.
2. There are many hand-curated sections.

Let's look at these points one by one.

Audiobooks

First, the top-menu navigation has Audiobooks *right next* to eBooks. More importantly, when I visited the site, there was a huge banner in the middle of the home page celebrating Audiobook Month:

Learn and listen: a Black Lives Matter reading list

View all

Further down, there's a whole section dedicated to audio hot new releases:

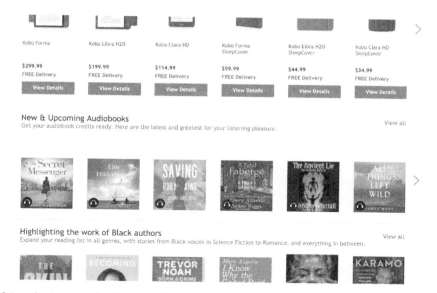

This relative emphasis on audio suggests that Kobo is looking to push audio sales more than any other store—probably because audiobooks have become a strong income channel for them. So if you're already having some success with your e-books on Kobo and *haven't* turned them into audiobooks yet, you know what to do.

Human curation

See the "Learn and listen: a Black Lives Matter reading list" and the "Highlighting the work of Black authors" sections above? These are *human-curated* sections, i.e., sections that display a list of books the Kobo merchandising team personally curated.

And that's the case for the majority of the carousel sections you'll see on Kobo—aside from the traditional Bestsellers, Trending Now, and New Releases sections, which are algorithmically ordered by sales.

Moreover, the Kobo store has huge sections highlighting just *one* book or deal:

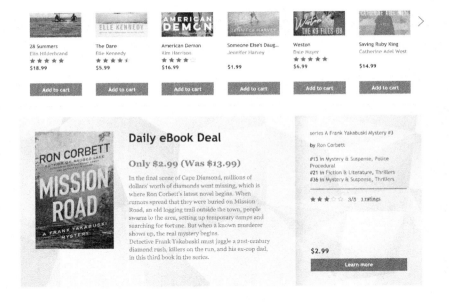

That's a prime piece of real estate—and it's also curated by Kobo's merchandising team.

So what's the *number-one thing* you can do to boost your sales on Kobo? Attract the attention of the merchandising team. And the best way to do that is by selling well, of course. (But that's a chicken-and-egg problem.)

Another good tip is to go to conferences. Even though the merch team usually won't be there, representatives from Kobo Writing Life often will, and they can help point you in the right direction.

Finally, there's one surefire way to get your books *considered* for inclusion in these hand-curated sections: the Promotions tab.

Applying for promotions

If you distribute to Kobo via Kobo Writing Life, you'll see that you have a Promotions tab in your dashboard. That's where the Writing Life team will inform you about new promotions the stores are running and how to apply to them.

As far as I know, there's no way to get e-mail alerts when a new promotion is added, so you'll need to log in often to find out about new ones. Some promotions will require you to drop your price, or even make the book free for a period of time, but it's definitely worth it.

If you get that promotion, make the most of it! Drive some Facebook or BookBub ads to your book during the promotion period, and let your list know about it. How successful your book is during the promotion might well determine if the merch team will consider it for *future* promotions.

If you don't distribute to Kobo via Writing Life but through an aggregator instead, check whether that aggregator has any special opportunities on Kobo that you could take part in. Draft2Digital is often invited to recommend authors or books for special promotions these stores run, so if you distribute through them you should try to meet with one of their reps (you'll find them at most conferences) so they have you on their radar.

Now that you know how visibility works on the Kobo store, it's time to look into—you guessed it—their search algorithm!

Kobo's search algorithm

Just as I did for Apple Books and Google Play Books, I'm going to decrypt how the search algorithm of the Kobo store works. In other words, I'll try to find out how Kobo decides which books to present (and in what order) when readers search for something specific on the store.

Note: since Canada is Kobo's biggest market, all the screenshots below are from the kobo.com/ca/store. But the same analysis applies to all Kobo country stores.

Of course, the best way to understand how a search algorithm works is to do a simple search, like "Victorian romance."

There are two main things that stand out to me when I run this search:

1. All the books on the first page of the results have either "Victorian Romance" or "A Victorian Romance" as the *subtitle* of the book.
2. Kobo shows a "Sort by" drop-down menu that lets the reader choose how to order the results. The preset default is "Bestseller," which would indicate that the books in the results are ordered by the number of sales.

Let's run a few more searches to confirm these hypotheses.

Keyword match in the title, subtitle, or author name

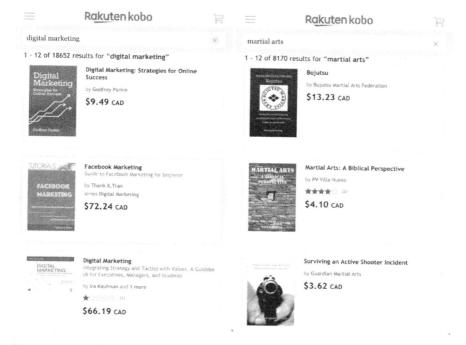

These two nonfiction searches give us a lot more info about keyword matches. Here, none of the books have the keyword in their subtitle. *However,* the keyword is present in either:

· the title
· the author name
· the series title

What's more, there's no particular order—which suggests that Kobo treats keyword matches in the title, subtitle, author name, or series title equally, and that the books that *have* such a match are then listed in the results by number of sales.

All about exact matches

When talking about keyword matches, it's important to specify whether we're talking about a "phrase match" or an "exact match."

For an exact match to happen, the text in the results must be *identical to the search query.* Phrase matches are more flexible and include instances in which the words are in a different order, singular vs. plural, or part of a longer phrase.

To understand the importance a search engine grants to exact matches (vs. just phrase matches), you can run two very similar searches—the only difference being the order of the words. And then you can see what happens:

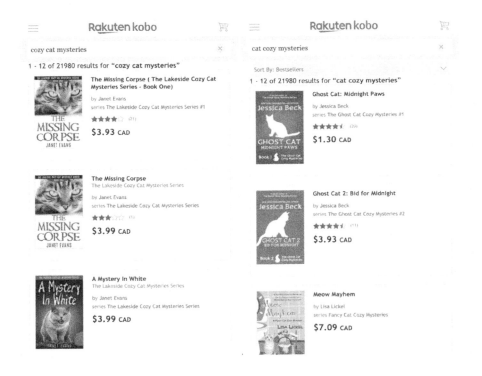

What these searches clearly show is that Kobo only values *exact matches.* If you don't have "cozy cat mystery" (exactly in this order) in either your title, subtitle, series title, or author name, your book won't show up in searches for that particular keyword phrase.

Seems a bit weird, right? Well, let's look at more examples.

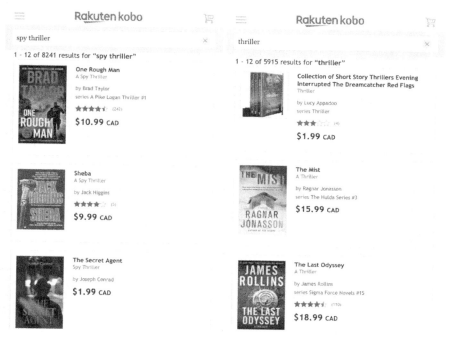

From these two searches, we can more clearly tell how Kobo brings the importance of exact matches to a whole other level. Let me explain.

The word "thriller" is included in the phrase "spy thriller," right? So if Kobo gave phrase matches *any* importance, then presumably the books showing up for "spy thriller" would show up for "thriller" as well. And since the results are ordered by "Bestseller," we'd see the highest-selling books first.

And yet, here's what we get if we look at the book ranking number one for "thriller":

Collection of Short Story Thrillers Evening Interrupted The Dreamcatcher Red Flags
Thriller

by Lucy Appadoo
series Thriller

Synopsis

Caterina is totally in lust with her boyfriend, Arthur, and she hopes that their one night of bliss will draw them closer. However, her hope is dashed when a surprise intruder interrupts their romantic interlude and wreaks havoc on their evening together. Then a new discovery shakes Caterina's world, and she starts to question her beliefs about herself. It is a night of terror for Caterina who wishes to protect Arthur and herself from the intruder, but will anyone survive in the end?

Aurora Mannindo, a 21-year old social work student, dreams of working with hospital patients in therapeutic care, but first, she has to get through her final work placement at a homeless shelter for men. For Aurora, it's the placement from hell. Her days are filled with red tape and paperwork, and several of the clients—what the staff call "Red Flag Clients"—are overtly threatening. Two, in particular, Marcus and David, seem to go out of their way to menace her. When her driver's license disappears the week Marcus is about to leave the shelter, Aurora begins to fear for her life. To save her best

Q Preview Now

⤓ Save Preview

★ ★ ★ ⯨ ☆ (4)

#12741 in Fiction & Literature, Action & Adventure
#22643 in Fiction & Literature, Thrillers
#30711 in Mystery & Suspense, Thrillers

↓

About this book

And here's the book ranking number one for "spy thriller":

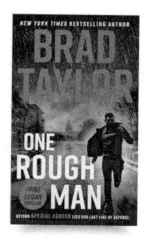

One Rough Man
A Spy Thriller

by Brad Taylor
series A Pike Logan Thriller #1

Synopsis

The first Pike Logan novel from *New York Times* bestselling author Brad Taylor.

They call it the Taskforce. Commissioned at the highest level of the U.S. government. Protected from the prying eyes of Congress and the media. Designed to operate outside the bounds of U.S. law. Trained to exist on the ragged edge of human capability.

Pike Logan was the most successful operator on the Taskforce, his instincts and talents unrivaled—until personal tragedy permanently altered his outlook on the world. Pike knows what the rest of the country might not want to admit: The real threat isn't from any nation, any government, any terrorist group. The real threat is one or two men, controlled by ideology, operating independently, in possession of a powerful weapon.

Buried in a stack of intercepted chatter is evidence of two such men. The transcripts

Q Preview Now

⤓ Save Preview

★ ★ ★ ★ ☆ (242)

#253 in **Fiction & Literature**, **Action & Adventure**
#731 in **Fiction & Literature**, **Thrillers**
#1049 in **Mystery & Suspense**, **Thrillers**

About this book

 498 Pages   🕐 **10 - 11** Hours to read   📖 **135k** Total words

Notice anything? *One Rough Man* has a ton more reviews and a much higher ranking than the short stories collection. Which means it sells *a lot better*. Yet it clearly ranks lower for the "thriller" search.

So I dug a bit further, and it looks like while Kobo does include phrase matches in their search results, those will show up after all the *exact* matches—regardless of how well they sell. In other words, here's how their search ranking algorithm probably works:

- First, it finds all the exact matches (in title, subtitle, series title, and author name) and orders those by sales.
- Then it finds all the phrase matches, orders those by sales, and displays them *below* the exact matches.

At the end of the day, this means that you'll have your best chance at ranking high for a given keyword or phrase if you have an *exact* keyword match.

It's keyword stuffing time! Or is it?

Now, I hesitated to include these chapters on how search works on the different wide stores—simply because it unveils how easy it is to *game* some of them. But I hope you'll realize this is not only an unethical strategy, but also an unsustainable one.

As these stores grow, they'll inevitably change their search. So the purpose of this chapter (and the previous ones) is *not* to get you to stuff your titles and subtitles with keywords, but to help you understand how to carry this analysis on your own in the future, as these stores evolve and develop more effective search algorithms.

28

To preorder or not to preorder

You might be wondering what this chapter on preorders is doing in the wide marketing section of this book. Partly it's because I didn't think it would fit anywhere else. And more importantly, it's because preorders can play an important role for visibility on non-Amazon retailers, particularly Apple Books and Kobo.

Preorders are so powerful on these retailers because a preorder sale counts twice toward best seller ranks:

- On Apple Books, once at the moment of the sale and once at launch
- On Kobo, twice at the moment of the sale

This means that preorders make it twice as easy to climb to the top of the rankings if you promote effectively on those platforms. Now, you might be wondering: *what about Amazon?* Can you use preorders in a similar way to nail your next book launch on the giant e-retailer?

The short answer is no. The long one's below. :)

Amazon: No country for preorders

The first thing to know about Amazon preorders is that they only count once toward the Best Seller ranks. Amazon factors them as a normal sale *at the time of the preorder*. In other words, preorders on Amazon don't offer any ranking boosts at launch (unless you manage to concentrate all your preorder sales right before the launch).

That's where the main issue lies. As you might already know, the most important period in a book's Amazon lifespan is the thirty days *after* launch. That's when you want to secure your sales by mobilizing and compounding all your promotion channels: your mailing list, social networks, price promotion, advertising, etc.

So if you run an Amazon preorder and tell your mailing list about it, you are effectively *stealing* sales away from launch week—right when they're the most valuable.

Sure, the sales you get from promoting the preorder to your fans could boost it in the rankings. However, there's some speculation that preorder sales count less on the Popularity list. Effectively, this means that Amazon grants your preorder less visibility in its search results (and e-mail recommendations) than it would if the book were *published*.

So not only are you stealing sales away from launch week, you're also getting less visibility from Amazon for those sales. Amazon is far from a promised land for preorders.

The solution? Keep your preorders exclusively wide

The contrast in terms of preorder friendliness between Amazon and Apple Books or Kobo has led many authors to use a simple strategy: they keep their preorders exclusive to the wide stores. The benefits of this strategy are obvious:

- You don't steal Amazon visibility from launch week.
- You benefit from the other retailers' added visibility for preorders.

- You have a product *exclusive* to these retailers, making it all the more attractive to their merchandising teams.

This is something I've preached for a while. That said, several authors got in touch with me to mention that there *were* benefits to having preorders on Amazon that in some cases could outweigh the reduced visibility. Let's discuss them now.

When does it make sense to set up a preorder on Amazon?

Rapid-release series

Remember our chapter on rapid-releasing? Well, if you use that strategy, it could very well make sense to use preorders. See, if you're launching book one without a preorder on books two and three, it'll show up as a single book on Amazon. Even if you have the phrase "book one" in the title and the name of your series on the cover, it might not be immediately obvious to Amazon browsers that it's part of a series.

Having books two and three on preorder—linked to book one through a series collection page—will make it clear to readers that (1) this is a new series, and (2) the following books will come out shortly.

Building your Also Boughts

Another benefit to running Amazon preorders has to do with Also Boughts.

Without a preorder, it can take a couple of weeks after a new release for the Also Boughts list to get populated. With Amazon preorders (and with the right prelaunch promotion), the book can have a dozen or more relevant Also Boughts already tied to it at the time of release. In turn, this means that Amazon will be more efficient at recommending your book at launch.

Depending on where you are in your career (and on the book you're launching), this can be a powerful reason to use Amazon preorders. If you're already a high-selling author, trading some launch week sales in exchange for a solid set of Also Boughts at launch could definitely be worth it.

As you can see, there's no easy answer when it comes to preorders! I hope this clears up some of the mysteries around them and helps you decide on the right strategy for your next launch.

VI

The mailing list

Amazon, Apple Books, Google Play, Kobo ... all these stores are where most of your sales will come from. But the problem with retailers is that they don't give you access to your readers. You know you got a sale, but you don't know who bought it, nor if they read it. And more importantly, you can't tell that reader when your next book is coming out—you can only hope the retailer will let them know when you do.
Which is why you need a mailing list.

29

Mailing list providers

You have probably read that the mailing list is your "number-one marketing tool." I tend to agree with that—even in the days of almighty Amazon and Kindle Unlimited. So it's about time for us to delve into the topic of mailing lists, newsletters, and reader magnets.

Disclaimer: Some of the content in this section has been repurposed from my Reedsy Learning course "How to Set up and Grow Your Author Mailing List." That said, this chapter goes more in depth on advanced topics like list segmentation, list cleaning, and newsletter swaps. So even if you've taken the course already, keep reading!

Why do I even need a mailing list?

Imagine your first book is super successful and sells ten thousand copies in its first month. Now you want to release the second one in the series. How will your original ten thousand customers find out about it? If they're not in your mailing list, they probably won't.

Your author mailing list is the main tool you can use to build a long-lasting relationship with your readers, turning them into repeat buyers and unconditional fans. Every sale you make while your mailing list is not in place is a lost opportunity.

"But isn't e-mail dead?" Sure, the rise of social media and chat apps has

changed the way we communicate and lifted some weight from e-mail, but no, e-mail is far from dead. It is the one form of communication we *all* use, and the one largely favored by consumers when receiving business promotions.

Remember what I said about control?

You can't control Facebook. Authors with huge followings on their author page got majorly screwed when Facebook started making them pay to reach their followers.

You can't control Amazon. Authors relying on free promotions for visibility saw this tactic badly hindered when Amazon introduced Kindle Unlimited in 2014.

What *can* you control? That's right: your mailing list. So even if you're still far from publishing your book, don't wait—set up your mailing list right away. And the first step is to select a provider.

Choosing your mailing list provider

This is the first decision you'll make, and you don't want to make it lightly. It's possible to switch from one provider to another even after everything is set up, but in most cases it's a pain, and time you could devote to other stuff (e.g., writing). So let's take a look at the main e-mail marketing services authors use and compare them. I'll let *you* make the decision about which service is right for *you*.

Now, you might be surprised that Mailchimp isn't in the list of providers below. Mailchimp would have definitely been my number-one recommendation until 2019, but in that year they decided to change their pricing model, as well as their brand focus, and turned into a highly unattractive option for authors. So instead, my main recommendations are MailerLite, ConvertKit, and Flodesk.

Option 1: MailerLite

MailerLite is generally my go-to option when I want to set up a mailing list for an author client. It's intuitive, has nearly all the options you'd want from a mailing list provider, and better yet, it's free until you've grown your list to more than one thousand readers.

Subscribers	Emails / month	Monthly cost
1 - 1,000	12,000	Free ❓
1 - 1,000	Unlimited	$ 10
1,001 - 2,500	Unlimited	$ 15
2,501 - 5,000	Unlimited	$ 30
5,001 - 10,000	Unlimited	$ 50

MailerLite pricing

Even on the free plan, you get access to all the important MailerLite features, in particular:

Importing subscribers

- Creating sign-up forms to add to your website, books, etc.
- Segmenting your list into different groups
- Integrating MailerLite with BookFunnel
- Designing beautiful e-mails with images, GIFs, and even custom HTML
- Viewing and analyzing data such as open rates, click rates, engagement level per subscriber, etc.

- Setting up welcome automations (also known as autoresponders)

So it's a good risk-free solution to get started on. The only negative points are that:

1. It can become expensive if you have a big list ($140 per month for a list of thirty thousand subscribers).
2. They've been known to have deliverability issues in the past, and even though their server reputation should be well established by now, it's still not as solid as some of the pricier services like Constant Contact, ActiveCampaign, or ConvertKit.

Speaking of which, let's take a look at ConvertKit.

Option 2: ConvertKit

ConvertKit is a pretty different option from MailerLite. It's both targeted at and optimized for professional bloggers. So what's different?

Better sign-up forms

On MailerLite, sign-up forms look pretty basic (unless you start custom-coding them). ConvertKit allows you to easily generate different sign-up forms, track their conversion rates, and embed them anywhere on your blog with WordPress plugins. If you have several "reader magnet" offers (more on those below) or run regular webinars or giveaways, these options will save you a lot of time and trouble.

Better segmentation and automation

This functionality makes it easy to segment, or divide, your list by autotagging users: "clicked on X link," "downloaded Y infographic," "attended Z webinar," etc.

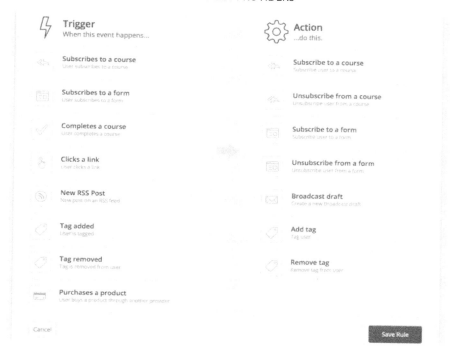

Then, ConvertKit allows you to build automations for each tag and offers a whole range of triggers for e-mails that aren't always available on MailerLite.

Limited design options

Design is where ConvertKit falls short. Their philosophy is that simple e-mails perform better than fancy templated ones, so their e-mail design tool doesn't have any bells and whistles. They justify this by explaining that simple e-mails get better deliverability (because there is less HTML) and feel more like e-mails from an actual human being. This is definitely debatable, but if you've found that simple text e-mails work better for your audience, then you won't miss the more advanced e-mail design possibilities ConvertKit doesn't offer.

Pricing

Another disadvantage: as opposed to MailerLite, ConvertKit doesn't have a "free forever" plan. Their first plan starts at twenty-nine dollars per month—and once your list grows beyond five thousand subscribers, you'll need to negotiate a custom plan, which will likely be double or triple what you'd pay on MailerLite.

ConvertKit pricing

That said, they do have a thirty-day refund policy, so you can always give them a try and see if their list segmentation and sign-up form features are worth the extra dollars.

Option 3: Flodesk

Flodesk is a newer service and sort of the opposite of ConvertKit: their focus is less on complex segmentation and multi-opt-in offers and more on simple yet beautiful e-mail design.

They offer a huge number of professional-looking, HTML-heavy templates, which allow you to create a proper brand feel and make your e-mails look special.

Learn to attract more
clients by being a *positive*
force in the world.

Flodesk templates

As such, they're mostly used by romance authors right now, though these templates could work just as well for self-help or health and well-being authors.

Flodesk also offers solid welcome automation triggers (similar to MailerLite), and nicely designed sign-up forms and pop-ups, however they're lacking in list segmentation options. In other words, if you write across several genres that have *some* crossover and use several reader magnets, you might quickly get stuck on Flodesk. As I mentioned, it's the opposite of ConvertKit.

There is *one* thing that makes Flodesk very attractive to authors with a big list: they have a *fixed pricing structure,* meaning your monthly cost doesn't grow with the size of your audience! Currently, that cost is at thirty-nine dollars a month, though if you search for "Flodesk review" on Google, you'll find several blogs offering an affiliate link that will lower that monthly price to just nineteen dollars a month.

I expect these prices to go up soon, so don't be surprised if you see higher numbers when you do your research.

That's it for my overview of service providers! Of course, these aren't the only three options. ActiveCampaign and Constant Contact can also be good (and expensive) choices—but you'll have to do your own research on those.

Once you've set up your mailing list, it's time to start bringing readers into it, which is what the next chapter is all about.

30

Reader magnets

By now, your mailing list should be set up and you should be ready to add your sign-up form to your website. So we're going to get to the million-dollar question: *"How do I get people to subscribe to my mailing list?"*

Let's think about it from the reader's perspective. What would make you, a reader, sign up for an author's newsletter? First, you'd have to come across their sign-up form somewhere. And then you'd need to be given a compelling enough reason to sign up. So the question becomes twofold:

1. How do I get readers to visit my website or landing page, which hosts my sign-up form?
2. How do I get this traffic to willingly sign up for my newsletter?

In this chapter, we're going to focus on that second question. Why start there? Well, let's say we solve challenge number one first, and suddenly you have tons of readers checking out your website every day. Great! But if you haven't solved the second challenge, only a tiny fraction of them will sign up to your mailing list—effectively wasting all the efforts you put into driving readers to your website in the first place.

Introducing Nick Stephenson's "reader magnets"

Now, the technique I'm going to discuss over the next several chapters is one developed by indie author Nick Stephenson—who also coined the term "reader magnets." So if you want to find out more after reading this, I recommend you take a look at his book *Reader Magnets: Build Your Author Platform and Sell More Books on Kindle*.[31]

So what's a reader magnet? Here's how Nick defines them: "Reader magnets are something of *value* that you give to your readers *in exchange* for an e-mail address."

Effectively, this means *offering a strong incentive* for people to sign up. Want an example?

Another one?

Bryan Hutchinson's blog

You get the gist. Readers need a good incentive to take action. If they land on your website and see a sign-up form that only says, "Please sign up to my newsletter to get updates about my future books," they're unlikely to sign up.

But if they see a sign-up form that says, "Get your free copy of my best-selling novel," they're much more likely to enter their e-mail addresses.

Ideas for reader magnets

More often than not, a reader magnet will be a short book (delivered via BookFunnel). But there are many other things you could try. Here's a list of some of the magnets I've seen authors use so far.

Fiction:

- Novella or short story set in the same universe as your main series
- Character backstory or deleted scenes
- Exclusive epilogue or alternate ending
- Free audiobook (you can use Authors Direct[32] to deliver it)
- Special art or illustrations related to the story (this can work particularly well for science-fiction and fantasy)

Nonfiction:

- Video course or training
- E-mail course (yes, our Reedsy Learning courses are *technically* magnets)
- Checklist, template, or cheat sheet
- Exclusive webinar
- Free audiobook
- Free software

Once you have the perfect magnet, make sure to feature it in as many places as possible, including:

- Your website, ideally front and center so as to capture as many visitors' e-mail addresses as possible (see the screenshot of Mark Dawson's website above)
- Your book, specifically its front and back matter, ideally right after "The End"
- Your Goodreads, Twitter, and Facebook bios

One really cool thing I don't see many authors doing is working their magnet *into* their book. For example, postapocalyptic author M. L. Banner created a real website for a fictional research institute in his book. And guess what? You can sign up for his particular reader magnet on that website. From my interview with him:[33]

> "I had a character in the book who was a scientist, and I thought it'd be really cool if he had this research institute. So I created a persona for him online: a G+ profile, a Twitter account, and a website for the CMER Institute. The key was really to think from my character's standpoint and see what I would do, in his place, to get the word out about this phenomenon [solar flares] that endangers the world.
>
> The beautiful thing about e-books is the connectivity—you can embed hyperlinks. So I linked to this CMERI website where my character actually offered a reader magnet: a free e-book called The

Apocalypse Survival Guide. *And I got over 1,200 downloads of that book. Some people even seem to believe that the CMERI is real, as I got a couple of media inquiries!"*

Delivering the reader magnet

Alright, so you have a reader magnet that's pulling readers into your list. The first step, before you do anything else, is to deliver on your reader magnet promise. In other words, if your reader magnet is a free novella, a reader signing up to your list will want to receive that novella in their inbox within seconds.

The simplest way to achieve that is to use BookFunnel.[34] I won't go into details (you can find more about them on their website), but just know that there are many types of e-readers and e-reading applications, and delivering the right device-specific file isn't always easy.

BookFunnel solves that problem. It creates a page for your book where readers can download the exact file they need. This is what the link in Nick Stephenson's welcome e-mail leads to:

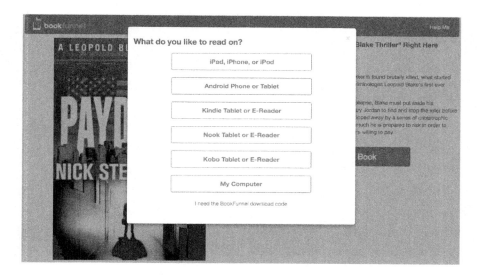

In other words, it provides a simple user experience for the reader and saves you from having to answer e-mails from readers who can't upload your files to their ten-year-old Kindle ...

Even better, BookFunnel seamlessly integrates with all the main e-mail marketing solutions, so they can send subscribers straight to your list when they download a magnet—but more about that in the next few chapters.

Testing your reader magnet

As you might have guessed from previous sections of this book, I'm a big advocate for *testing*. Many authors base their most important marketing decisions (like their cover designs or their reader magnets) on intuition and "whatever is working for other authors." And while that's a good starting point, nothing beats actual, methodical testing (if you can afford it).

I already mentioned how you should A/B test your book covers through Facebook ads. And we can apply the same advice to testing reader magnets.

Say I wanted to know whether readers in my niche would respond more to a free video course or a free cheat sheet. Well, I'd set up two Facebook lead ad campaigns, one promoting each magnet—with identical targeting—and see which one got me the cheapest cost per lead.

That's effort, sure, and it requires creating several magnets ... but what if you find out that one converts two times, three times, or even five times better than the other one? That's not an uncommon result. And surely growing your mailing list two to five times quicker every month is worth the trouble!

In fact, at the 2019 20Books Vegas conference, Mark Dawson mentioned a case study in which a popular romance author decided to do just that: she switched her magnet from a free book to a free exclusive epilogue. And guess what? Her mailing list grew from five thousand to thirty thousand followers. That's a growth of 500 percent by changing *one small thing*, with zero extra effort! So once you have a reader magnet that brings a few readers into your list every week, don't rest on your laurels. Instead ask, "Is there a magnet that would appeal to authors even more?" If so, put it together and test it. Or even better, survey your audience about what they'd like as a bonus for being in your mailing list, create it for them, and test it as a new magnet going forward!

31

Welcome automations

Using reader magnets to bring hundreds of readers to your mailing list every week is just the first step—and it's a worthless one if you don't *interact* with those readers afterwards.

That's what welcome automations—also known as e-mail sequences, workflows, or autoresponders—are for. Automations allow you to send e-mails as soon as the reader performs an action on your list (e.g., when they sign up for it by downloading your reader magnet). They're your first point of contact with the reader, and you know what they say about first impressions ...

The importance of welcome automations

Welcome automations are all the more relevant if you run ads for your magnet or if you run group giveaways. Someone who signs up for your magnet after reading the back matter of one of your books is probably already a fan of your writing (or a "warm lead" in marketing jargon). But if they sign up for it from a Facebook ad? Well, they'll likely come in knowing nothing about you. (They're "cold leads," in other words.)

And that's where a *good* welcome automation kicks in: it warms up those cold leads and turns them into loyal readers.

To sum up:

- Reader magnets turn casual browsers or readers of your book into mailing list subscribers.
- Welcome automations turn these new subscribers into fans.

So how do you go about nailing that awesome welcome automation? Let's look at some dos and don'ts.

Don't: Go for the hard sell

It can be tempting to send new subscribers a welcome e-mail with links to your entire catalog of books. After all, your mailing list exists to drive sales, right?

But let's say you're at a food market and all of the stalls are offering samples of their food. You approach one of them, pick up a sample, and (before you've even gotten the chance to stuff it in your mouth!) the merchant shoves the menu in your face—without any small talk or interest in whether you enjoyed the sample.

I'm guessing the merchant would come across as rather salesy, right? Well, that's exactly how you'll be perceived if you start your automation with a "buy my books" e-mail.

Instead, you want to create a *connection* with the reader. Ideally, your automation should strike a perfect balance between building a relationship (soft sell) and getting them to buy your books (hard sell).

A simple yet effective tactic is to offer a *second* magnet—like a second free story or novella. Since the reader won't be expecting it, it'll create sort of a "Wow, you're generous" moment. More importantly, if you use a subject line like "Another free story for you," you'll dramatically increase the chances of them opening the e-mail. And training readers to open your e-mails (and answer them) will in turn boost your deliverability down the line. Speaking of which ...

Do: Ask your readers a question

Including a question to your readers in the first e-mail of your welcome automation is an increasingly common tactic. It can be as simple as: "Which of my books (if any) have you already read?" or "What did you think of the last … movie?"

Keep the question simple (which means that you shouldn't ask them for in-depth feedback on your books or for a dissertation on the meaning of happiness). What you want is to maximize the number of people who'll get back to you. Tammi Labrecque, an expert on author mailing lists, gave a great talk about this at 20Books Vegas. When she discussed the "e-mail question," she summarized it perfectly: "A good first e-mail question is one that readers want to answer."

"Why would I ever want that? I have more than enough e-mails in my inbox already!" Maybe, but once a reader *answers* one of your e-mails, your sender address is automatically whitelisted in their inbox—meaning none of your future e-mails will go to spam or promotions boxes. And that's well worth the five minutes it'll take you to acknowledge their responses.

Note: If you don't know her yet, Tammi is the author of Newsletter Ninja,[35] *the ultimate book on building an active mailing list as an author. I can't recommend it enough if you want to, well, become a newsletter ninja.*

Do: Take inspiration from other authors

Whenever authors ask me what they should put in their welcome automation, how many e-mails they should include in the automation, at which frequency, etc., I tell them to sign up to as many other authors' newsletters as possible and take inspiration from them.

Granted, not everyone has welcome automations, and few authors keep them fresh and up to date. But I guarantee that if you sign up for five to ten newsletters from other authors, you'll receive at least two you can take inspiration from.

To get you started, I recommend some authors below whose automation games are on point:

- Erica Ridley (historical romance): Probably the most impressive author I know when it comes to e-mail marketing
- Mark Dawson (thrillers): You probably know him already. He offers *three books* as a reader magnet, and the subsequent automation lives up to the expectation.
- David Gaughran (writing and publishing nonfiction): Another name that's probably familiar. You can join his list by downloading his super-useful magnet, *Following*.

You'll find links to sign up to each of their newsletters in the endnotes.[36]

The great thing about automations is that they require very little further work from you once they're set up. They will automatically do the work of greeting readers for you and turning them first into customers and then into fans. Of course, you should periodically check the stats of your automation e-mails (open rates, click rates, etc.) and make small changes here and there to strengthen them even more.

32

List segmentation

As I mentioned, the great thing about automations is that they can put your e-mail marketing game on autopilot. As in, they'll *automatically* send e-mails based purely on your subscriber's actions.

The slight drawbacks to an e-mail automation, however, are that (1) you need to keep them updated (e.g., when you release a new book), and (2) they can feel pretty impersonal—if you're not segmenting your list well.

The importance of list segmentation

Not all readers are created equal. And not all subscribers are created equal, either.

As we saw in the last chapter, a reader who signed up to get your magnet from a Facebook ad will be very different from someone who signed up to your list from the back matter of one of your books. You can't treat these two readers equally.

Similarly, if you write in different series—let alone different genres—you can't treat their readers equally.

This is why you should *segment* your list. Segmentation ensures that you greet all these different groups of readers in the appropriate way. For example:

- **A Facebook ad reader:** "I hope you've been able to successfully download my free novella onto your favorite reading device. Once you've had a chance to read it, I'd love to have your thoughts on it!"
- **A reader from the back matter of a book in your Cocky Lovers series:** "Thank you again for joining my mailing list! You should have received an e-mail to download my free *Cockier Spaniel* novella. Now, I'm curious: who's your favorite character in the Cocky Lovers series so far?"
- **A reader from the back matter of a book in another series:** "Welcome to my reader group! I always like to send new readers a little welcome gift, so here's a link to download *Dark Panther*, a free novella set in the universe of my Carpathian Leopards series."

Of course, it goes without saying that the subsequent e-mails in the automation should be similarly personalized for their respective segments.

"That's great, but how do I go about segmenting my list?"

I'm glad you asked!

List segmentation basics

Segmenting a list is simple ... in theory. You just attach attributes, or tags, to your subscribers. Then you can segment them based on these tags.

For example, your sign-up form should probably have a hidden field for the reader's provenance:

- Facebook ads
- Back matter series A
- Back matter series B
- Website
- BookFunnel
- Etc.

If you use MailerLite, you can do this super easily by creating a new Field in the Subscribers section, then adding it as a hidden field on your sign-up form:

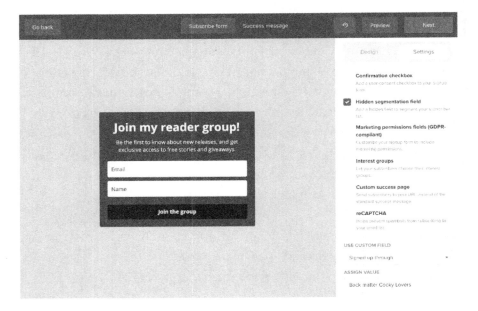

If you don't like hidden fields, you can also use MailerLite's group functions. For example, if you have two separate magnets on BookFunnel (*Cockier Spaniel* and *Dark Panther*), you could set up something like this:

1. Set up two new groups on MailerLite, called "Spaniel magnet" and "Panther magnet."
2. Connect the BookFunnel page for *Cockier Spaniel* to the Spaniel magnet group on MailerLite.
3. Connect the BookFunnel page for *Dark Panther* to the Panther magnet group on MailerLite.
4. Set up specific welcome automations for both groups, which, once finished, copy the subscriber over to your main group.
5. *Optional:* preclude people who've already received one automation from receiving the other.

This way, you make sure that people who download one of your two magnets get a welcome automation dedicated to that magnet and then join your main list.

You can go deeper with your segmentation by sending questions or polls to readers. For example, you could have one e-mail ask readers coming from one of your two series, "Which of my series have you already started reading?" Then you'd have three options for them: A, B, and both.

E-mail marketing systems like MailerLite then allow you to group, segment, and tag people based on what they click on. This is a good way to make sure you only send hyper-relevant information to your readers in the future.

Personalization vs. newsletter fatigue

Segmentation is a must to make sure you only send relevant stuff to your audience. But sometimes, *relevancy* isn't enough.

We live in a world where there are more and more authors every day. Not to mention that everyone's marketing game has risen. Almost all the full-time indie authors I know (and I know hundreds of them) have a newsletter, a magnet, an automation, and so on.

This means that, in a lot of commercial genres, readers tend to receive *a lot* of e-mails from authors they follow. As a result, they tend to open e-mails less and less. Some circles have started referring to this as "newsletter fatigue."

Personally, I think this problem is slightly overstated. Readers still look forward to their favorite authors' newsletters. You just need to make sure you're one of them.

And that's where personalization comes in. The more you can make your reader feel *special*, like you're talking to *them*, the higher the chances they'll look forward to your next e-mail.

One cool tool I recently came across in that respect is Bonjoro.[37] It allows you to send a personalized video greeting to your new subscribers and has integrations with all e-mail marketing services (MailerLite included).

Personal videos in e-mails are still rare, so that's one easy way to stand out and make sure your readers remember you. Remember: if you manage to get readers to engage with your *first* e-mail, you drastically increase the chances they'll open your future ones.

33

Cleaning your list

I briefly touched on e-mail deliverability in the previous chapters, but it's such an important topic that it warrants a chapter of its own.

What the heck is e-mail deliverability?

In a nutshell, e-mail deliverability refers to the proportion of e-mails you send that actually end up in the *inboxes* of your readers. See, depending on a number of factors, it's quite likely that a good percentage of your e-mails will end up in the spam folder or the Promotions tab. These are parts of the inbox readers rarely check out—which negatively impacts your open rates.

So how does an e-mail client like Gmail or Yahoo Mail decide which e-mails to classify as spam or a promotion? Well, it looks at two series of factors:

- Structural factors related to the sender's e-mail and IP address
- Conjunctural factors related to the e-mail itself

You'll probably have heard about the second one already: if you include the word "free" in your subject line, or if your e-mail contains lots of images or HTML formatting, then e-mail clients often consider it a promotional e-mail.

That said, these conjunctural factors are easy to test: simply send an A/B-tested newsletter with one version containing HTML formatting and the other version in plain text. Or one version with images and the other one without.

It's the structural factors that are more worrying, as they're a lot harder to reverse.

Keeping a clean mailing list

See, all the e-mails you send come from the same e-mail address, or domain. That address/domain is constantly evaluated and rated by receiving e-mail clients (Gmail, Yahoo Mail, etc.) based on how the recipients react to it.

For example, say that an important portion (e.g., 5 percent) of your Gmail subscribers mark one of your e-mails as spam. This will negatively impact your e-mail address's score in the eyes of Google. The more negative signals, the lower your score will become. And as it goes down, so does your deliverability.

To give an opposite example: let's say a vast portion of subscribers tend to interact with your first e-mail (e.g., respond to it). This signals to e-mail clients that your address is to be trusted (and that it's probably not related to promotions or marketing), since people are replying to it. Your score will go up, and so will the deliverability of your future e-mails. That's why including a question in the first e-mail of your welcome automation is so crucial. (Did I mention that already?)

So how do you keep that score up? It's simple (in theory): you make sure to only send relevant e-mails to subscribers who are genuinely interested in receiving them.

In other words, you make sure to always keep a *clean* mailing list. A big part of that is having proper segmenting in place, but segmenting is not enough. Sometimes, keeping a mailing list *clean* requires a proper purge.

Purging subscribers

The act of purging subscribers is exactly what it sounds like: you massively unsubscribe segments of your list that are, or could be, negatively affecting its deliverability.

It's not something to be done lightly: after all, it costs money and effort to acquire a mailing list subscriber. But it also costs money to *maintain* your list—e-mail marketing services charge you more as your list gets bigger.

If a subscriber hasn't opened any of your past twenty e-mails, you're effectively paying to keep a dormant person in your list. Not only that, but the more dormant subscribers you have, the *lower* your open rates will drop. And low open rates are in itself a negative signal for e-mail deliverability.

To sum up, you *really* don't want dormant subscribers on your list. So what's the solution? Should you just cull everyone from your list who hasn't opened any of your last twenty e-mails?

No. First, you should try to wake them up by giving them one last chance to interact with your e-mails. Send them a blunt e-mail explaining that, unless they take action (e.g., click or answer), you'll unsubscribe them from your mailing list.

In most cases, you'll only manage to wake up a tiny percentage of dormants, but that's better than nothing!

The danger of giveaways and group promos

Giveaways and group bundles (e.g., through BookFunnel, Prolific Works or BookSweeps[38]) are common methods of building a mailing list for cheap. The only issue with them is that you run the risk of building a list of "freebie seekers."

And guess what? Freebie seekers tend to become dormant very quickly after they get their freebie.

So you should have a safeguard in place to *automatically* cull them from your list if they go dormant. You can easily achieve this through proper segmenting and automation: just make sure to put all of them into a group or segment, and then deliver a specific welcome automation to that segment. At the end of the automation, just automatically unsubscribe all of the people who have not opened or clicked on your last few e-mails.

You now know the basics of mailing list hygiene. If e-mail marketing is going to play an important part for you, then I recommend you further research the topic, and in particular, purchase Tammi Labrecque's book *Newsletter Ninja*.

34

Newsletter swaps

A mailing list is the most efficient and sustainable way to build a direct line of communication with your readers. But the benefits don't end there—it can also allow you to reach *new* readers. How? Through newsletter swaps.

The magic of newsletter swaps

Say you're releasing a new book or running a price promotion, and you want to get *eyeballs* on it. What are your options?

A mailing list or an existing audience on social media are the obvious places to start. But these are readers who *already* know about you. So how do you reach *new* readers?

Well, you can always advertise, either directly on Amazon or through social media (Facebook and BookBub, primarily). You can also buy placements (another form of advertisement) on sites and newsletters with a preexisting audience. We call these "price promotion sites," and I'll go into those in more detail in the next section.

These are all solid options, and I've used all of them successfully in the past year for clients. *They all work.* But there's one thing that trumps the others: the newsletter swap.

If you're not familiar with the concept, it's quite straightforward. You promote another author's book in your newsletter to your mailing list, and in exchange they promote yours to *their* mailing list. In other words, you *swap* mailing list announcements—generally for a new release or a price promo.

Why is this so powerful? Because you are introduced to a whole new audience by someone who *has already earned that audience's trust.* Let's say you're a huge Brandon Sanderson fan. Now imagine that he tweets about a book saying it was the best epic fantasy he'd read this year. You'd go buy it immediately, right?

Well, that's effectively what a newsletter swap achieves. Readers get your book recommended to them by an author they already love.

"That's great, but how do I do this swap thing?"

It's simple: you *make friends.* A mailing list is probably the most precious thing any author can have. It's their gateway to their readers, their fans. It's their direct line of communication, and it can get damaged if they use it too often or not often enough—even if they don't use it to send relevant stuff.

In other words, authors are not going to put *your* book in their newsletters unless they are 100 percent certain their audience is going to *like* your book. This implies that they have either already read your book, or that they know you well enough to trust that everything you write is good and will appeal to their readers.

In both cases, it means you need to build a relationship with that author.

"But I'm sure that some authors must be willing to swap newsletters with strangers without first checking out their books." Yes, but an author who doesn't vet a newsletter swap most likely doesn't care one bit about their readers. Are those the kind of newsletters you want to get on? Probably not.

So how do you build a relationship with an author the *right* way? Well, you start by reading their books. Then—*if* you enjoy them—you review them. And then you get in touch with the author, both as a fellow author and a fan.

You can also join online groups of indie authors in your genre. It's a great way to start interacting and making real friends in those groups. And the most effective way, of course, is to attend conferences and meet people in person.

Now, you should make sure that the authors you're looking to swap with have a newsletter, and that it's more or less the same size as yours. If you're just starting out in a genre, don't ask an indie author who's selling a million copies a month to swap newsletters with you—you'll just come across as greedy and unprofessional.

Keep swaps in your genre

All in all, I see newsletter swaps as the strongest, most reliable, and most scalable (not to mention ROI-efficient, since it's technically free) marketing tactic right now to bring *relevant traffic* to a book.

That said, this particular method depends on relationships built over time. So it's not something you can activate right off the bat like a Facebook or Amazon ad—which is why ads will remain just as relevant next year as they were last year.

More importantly, newsletter swaps can become a double-edged weapon if you don't *keep them in your genre.*

If you write cozy mysteries, for example, and just happen to have a good friend who writes dark horror, *do not* swap newsletters with them. Don't even let them mention your book to their audience. If you do, you'll most likely end up with a wave of negative reviews. And even in the off chance that their horror fans discover the charm of cozies and enjoy your book, you'd instantly pollute your Also Boughts—and we know how hard that is to reverse. So for the sake of clean and relevant Also Boughts, keep the swaps in your genre!

If you're just starting to build your list and are not ready to swap with other authors just yet, don't despair. You can still get your book in front of genre lovers by running discount promotions and buying advertising spots in book promotion newsletters. That's what we call "price promotions," and it's what the next section is all about.

VII

Price promotions

By now, we've covered everything you need to know and have if you want to sell books: the right mindset, the right product for the right market, an optimized Amazon (and other retailer) presence, and a mailing list.
It's now time to look at channels to bring traffic to your books. And the most popular and effective one, to date, is running a price promotion.

35

What is a price promotion?

Have you noticed how stores are swarmed by shoppers as soon as the sales season begins? Well, the same principle applies to books. If you want to increase the discoverability of your product, discounting it for a short period of time (and promoting this sale) is the best way to do it. That's what we call a price promotion.

"Sure, I might get more sales if I discount my book, but since I make less money on each sale, does it really matter?" In a word: yes. If you're selling on Amazon (or Apple Books or Kobo or Google Play, etc.), a sale isn't *just* worth the money you get out of it—it also has an impact on your book's ranking in search results and best seller lists, which in turn will trigger even more sales.

That's the whole objective of running a price promotion: hitting enough visibility spots on retailers that, when the promotion is over, your book will continue to sell well for a few days—at full price.

Promoting your discounted book

Now, a decade ago, setting a book to free or $0.99 on the Kindle Store was enough to fetch thousands of sales or downloads. Not only is that not the case today, but if you don't actively promote your discounted or free book, you might not even see *any* increase in sales.

Price promotions don't magically sell books. However, they do make it *incredibly easier* to market a book.

First, discounts have a psychological impact on readers: you might not take a chance on a new author if their book is selling at $4.99, but you probably wouldn't mind downloading their book for free on your Kindle, or getting it for $0.99.

More importantly, discounting your book gives you access to a whole suite of tools and sites that can help you market it. We call them price promotion sites.

The power of price promotion sites

In a nutshell, price promotion sites are websites or newsletters (or both) that:

· Have a preestablished reader base
· Regularly advertise discounted or free books to that reader base

As an author, you can pay to acquire a spot on their site or newsletter to advertise *your* book to their readers.

The most famous one is BookBub, but it's infamously hard to grab a spot on it as an indie writer. You need dozens (if not hundreds) of reviews, a lot of luck, and many tries—but don't worry, there's a whole chapter coming on BookBub.

In any case, there are hundreds of *smaller* price promo sites with a similar model to BookBub that are much easier to advertise on. You'll still need a good number of reviews (ten to fifteen for most non-BookBub sites), and make sure to submit to them several weeks in advance, as they tend to be booked out. But by compounding several of them and running some ads of your own, you can get close to replicating the effects of a BookBub Featured Deal.

Now, not all these sites are worth it. Some have audiences too small or not engaged enough to make a difference, while others are genre specific. It can be hard to find them all and even harder to determine which you should book. This is why we created a handy little resource at Reedsy: a directory of price promo sites classified into tiers.[39] If you're short on budget, stick to tiers I and II: these are the most likely to offer you a positive return on investment.

All this sounds great on paper, but you might be wondering exactly how to plan and execute a price promotion. Well, the next chapter offers some practical examples.

36

Price promotion example

Now that you know the basics and the philosophy behind price promotions, it's time to look into a fictional example of what a successful price promo could look like.

For this purpose, we're imagining that you have a *series* with at least three books. (If you only have one book, this example is still valid; just ignore the parts about books two and three.)

```
Disclaimer: this is not a new strategy or anything; in fact I'm
"stealing" a lot of it from David Gaughran's usual advice around
price promotions.
```

Step 1: Decide on the discounts

Of course, how deep you discount depends on how aggressive you want the price promotion to be. The more you discount, the more visibility the books will get—but that doesn't necessarily mean you'll make more money, as each sale will bring you less.

If your goal is to reach as many new readers as possible, I think it's worth being extra aggressive. So here's what I'd do.

If your books are in Kindle Unlimited:

- Make book one free for five days (free KDP Select promotion).
- Discount book two to $0.99 for five days (Countdown Deal).
- Discount book three to $1.99 for five days (Countdown Deal).

If your books are wide:

- Discount books one and two to $0.99 for seven days.
- Discount book three to $1.99 for seven days.

Why the difference? As you may recall from the chapter on Kindle Unlimited, books enrolled in KU often make you more money through borrows than through sales. So you shouldn't be afraid of deep-discounting and sacrificing sales dollars.

Step 2: Research price promotion sites

Head to our list of book promotion sites, and note down (in a spreadsheet):

- All sites in tier I
- All sites in tier II that cater to your genre

Next, visit each price promo site and check for their nearest availability in terms of dates. You'll see that several of them (e.g., Robin Reads) need to be booked several weeks in advance. Add those dates to the spreadsheet.

Step 3: Decide on the dates and book the promo sites

Once you have that info, you can pick your dates and verify that all your target price promotion sites will actually be bookable for those dates.

Then it's just a matter of booking them (i.e., paying for the feature). You should direct most of your promos to book one, but you can get a couple for book two as well. For example, in the KU strategy, it might be a good idea to get a Freebooksy for book one and a Bargain Booksy for book two.

Step 4: Set up your advertising budgets

The objective of this aggressive price promo is to get your books *as high up* in the ranks as possible—which means that you want to concentrate your ad spend during the dates of the promo.

Ideally, you want your sales during your promotion period to follow a bell curve. For that, you should spread your promotion sites and advertising spend mostly evenly throughout the five or seven days—with a small focus on days two and three.

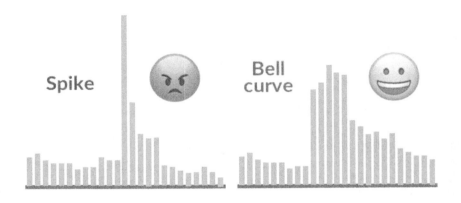

"But won't a big spike get me higher in the rankings than a bell curve?"

Yes, but only temporarily. Also, Amazon will see a spike as an anomaly—or worse, as a ranking manipulation, causing your fall afterwards to be all the greater.

"Wait, then how would you divide up the budget for something like this?"

Glad you asked! Here's what your money spend could look like with a budget of $1,000:

	Day 1	Day 2	Day 3	Day 4	Day 5	Total
Price promo sites	$50	$75	$100	$75	$50	$350
Facebook ads	$50	$75	$100	$75	$50	$350
BookBub ads	$50	$75	$100	$75	$50	$350
Total	**$150**	**$225**	**$300**	**$225**	**$150**	**$1,050**

Step 5: Draft Facebook and BookBub ads in advance of the promo

You've got only a few days to make the most of this, so you want to prepare your ads in advance. Most advertising platforms will only push your ads live after they've been reviewed and approved. The last thing you want is to set up ads on day one of your promo and see them go live on day three.

Luckily, you can *schedule* ads on both BookBub and Facebook. So you should draft and plan them several days in advance. And if it's your first time creating ads on those platforms—or if you need to brush up on your skills—make sure you read the next section of this book carefully.

Again, your ads should point mostly to book one, but you can also take advantage of *series* ads and point to your *series collection* page on Amazon.

Step 6: Schedule a newsletter (or several)

If you have a mailing list, you should make sure to leverage it during the promo as well. Even if a good chunk of your subscribers has already read your books, they might forward your newsletter to their friends (who probably haven't).

If you have a mailing list with more than five thousand subscribers, it's worth splitting your subscribers in two and sending two e-mails (on days two and three, for example), so as not to create a spike.

And if you have friends in the author community, now is also the time to ask for newsletter swaps!

Step 7: Monitor your sales during the promo and adjust accordingly

At this point, if you've done all your homework correctly, you won't have much work left to do *during* the promo—aside from adjusting your ads.

Monitor your sales, and increase (or decrease) your budgets accordingly to make sure you get to the top of your categories.

And that's it for this price promo example! If you apply it, you should see some decent results on your first try. More importantly, the more price promos you run, the better the results will get, as you'll garner more experience on which promo sites and ad platforms perform best for your books.

37

How to get a BookBub Featured Deal

Getting featured on most price promotion sites or newsletters is relatively easy, as long as you plan your promotion in advance and have a good ten to fifteen (or more) reviews on Amazon. There is one exception, though, and a mighty one: BookBub.

Whether you're working on your first book or have published dozens of them, my guess is you've probably heard of BookBub, if not used it as a reader. In a publishing world increasingly dominated by Amazon, BookBub has emerged and established itself as a company offering a solid marketing alternative to authors and publishers—and has allowed many of them to hit coveted best seller lists through their famous Featured Deals.

BookBub was one of the earliest price promotion sites, and has since grown to become the largest and most effective one—by a stretch. As such, it has also become the most coveted, by both indie authors and traditional publishers, making it *nearly* impossible for new authors to even get a Featured Deal with them.

Why a dedicated chapter on BookBub Featured Deals, then? Because if you do manage to get one, it'll be the single biggest boost to your sales you'll ever get, and will propel you to the top of your category rankings. More importantly, while it is undeniably hard to get that Deal, you can do a good number of things to make it a lot more likely. But first, let's take a look at how these Deals work.

How do Bookbub Featured Deals work?

For every one of their forty-two genre categories, BookBub sends daily and weekly e-mails to readers (subscribed to that genre) featuring discounted and/or free books. Getting a spot among those discounted or free books is what a Featured Deal is all about. But before we go into what it takes to achieve that, let's talk money.

How much does a Featured Deal cost?

First, something quite important: it doesn't cost you *anything* to *submit* your title for a Featured Deal. You only pay if your deal is accepted. Now, when that happens, on top of the cost of the bottle of champagne you'll open to celebrate it, you'll have to pay BookBub for the feature.

The cost of a Featured Deal depends on several factors:

· The price at which your book will be discounted (the more you discount, the cheaper the Deal)
· The BookBub genre category you submit your book in (and the expected performance of BookBub newsletters in this genre)
· Whether you're getting a US Featured Deal or an international-only one (US ones are much more expensive)

You can view a list of all prices, based on these factors, on the BookBub website. Here's a screenshot of the 2020 prices for US Featured Deals:

Category	Subscribers	BookBub fee by Book Price					Free Book Stats	Discounted Book Stats
		Free	<$1	$1-$2	$2-$3	$3+	Avg Dwnlds	Avg Sold
Crime Fiction	3,330,000+	$603	$876	$1,577	$2,190	$3,066	30,200	2,250
Historical Mysteries	2,170,000+	$571	$830	$1,494	$2,075	$2,905	19,000	1,900
Cozy Mysteries	2,010,000+	$571	$830	$1,494	$2,075	$2,905	32,000	2,350
Contemporary Romance	1,880,000+	$560	$814	$1,466	$2,035	$2,849	26,200	2,050
Women's Fiction	1,660,000+	$557	$810	$1,458	$2,025	$2,835	25,400	2,350
Historical Fiction	2,330,000+	$552	$802	$1,444	$2,005	$2,807	19,600	2,550
Biographies and Memoirs	2,460,000+	$509	$740	$1,332	$1,850	$2,590	20,000	1,900
Cooking	1,190,000+	$479	$696	$1,253	$1,740	$2,436	21,500	1,700
Thrillers	2,490,000+	$476	$692	$1,246	$1,730	$2,422	23,100	1,850
Psychological Thrillers	2,060,000+	$442	$642	$1,156	$1,605	$2,247	21,100	1,650
Erotic Romance	870,000+	$434	$630	$1,134	$1,575	$2,205	17,100	1,300
Literary Fiction	2,410,000+	$412	$598	$1,077	$1,495	$2,093	25,600	1,950
Science Fiction	1,450,000+	$409	$594	$1,070	$1,485	$2,079	18,200	1,450
Historical Romance	1,330,000+	$402	$584	$1,052	$1,460	$2,044	15,200	1,600
Action and Adventure	1,840,000+	$385	$560	$1,008	$1,400	$1,960	19,500	1,400
Advice and How-To	1,050,000+	$385	$560	$1,008	$1,400	$1,960	10,800	1,300
History	1,550,000+	$372	$540	$972	$1,350	$1,890	12,700	1,400
Christian Nonfiction	790,000+	$372	$540	$972	$1,350	$1,890	9,500	1,000
Fantasy	1,490,000+	$355	$516	$929	$1,290	$1,806	19,300	1,400
Romantic Suspense	1,320,000+	$340	$494	$890	$1,235	$1,729	20,500	1,950
American Historical Romance	940,000+	$340	$494	$890	$1,235	$1,729	14,800	950
General Nonfiction	1,920,000+	$324	$470	$846	$1,175	$1,645	13,400	1,250

2020 US BookBub Featured Deals

BookBub's criteria for selecting books to feature

BookBub's official criteria to accept Featured Deal submissions are pretty clear. According to their own website,[40] your title should be:

- Free or discounted by at least 50 percent
- The best deal available. The book can't have been offered at a lower price anywhere in the past ninety days.
- Error free
- A limited-time offer (except for free promotions, in which they do accept perma-free books)
- A full-length book, with a minimum number of pages (150 for novels, 100 for nonfiction)
- No novellas or short stories

- Widely available, i.e., at least on one major retailer in either the US or the UK—and the more, the merrier

Lastly, BookBub will not feature the same book from an indie author more than once every six months. Nor will they feature the same indie author more than once every thirty days. But more on that later.

Now, these are the *minimum requirements* for a deal to be submitted to BookBub. Meeting these requirements certainly doesn't guarantee your deal will be accepted by their editorial team and featured in a newsletter—far from it. Which brings us to the following million-dollar question ...

How can I maximize my chances of getting a Featured Deal?

In recent years, BookBub Featured Deals have become harder to get for indie authors. Some say their editorial team favors deals from traditional publishers—though that has been formally denied by the company.

One thing is sure: BookBub bases most of its decisions on *data*. After years of serving deals to millions of readers and watching how these readers react, they have a pretty good idea of what will work (or won't) for their audience.

BookBub's selection process for Featured Deals also relies heavily on human curation. They have an editorial team for every genre that goes through the submissions and handpicks the Deals to feature every day.

With that in mind, let's look at how you can boost your chances of getting that coveted Featured Deal. Here are my top nine tips:

Tip 1: Subscribe to BookBub's newsletters in your genre

If you want to get a Deal in a genre, the first step is to understand what BookBub's curators in that genre are looking for. And you can get a glimpse of that by simply signing up as a reader to their newsletters in that genre. Check out the books they feature, and analyze what they have in common. (What do the covers look like? What are the price points? How many reviews do the books have? Etc.)

Tip 2: Make sure your book has an appropriate number of reviews

From BookBub's blog:[41]

> *"Reader reviews and ratings help our editors get a sense of how readers have responded to your book, and they are a crucial element of the selection process. [...] We recommend browsing through the books we're featuring in your category to get a sense of what a competitive number of positive reviews is for that genre."*

This goes back to my advice above: check out the kind of books they feature, and note the usual number of reviews. There's no sense in applying for a Featured Deal until you have a similar number of reviews.

```
Note: For this reason, it's highly unrealistic (read: a waste of
time) to apply for a BookBub Featured Deal for a new release, as
you won't have any reviews when submitting it. For new releases,
BookBub has a separate product you could try: Featured New
Releases.
```

Tip 3: Polish your product pages on all retailers

What do BookBub's curators look at when evaluating a deal? The same thing that readers will: the book's information on retailer pages. Their goal is the same as yours: selling as many books as possible. So they want to make sure that the books they feature are optimized to drive sales.

In particular, this means:

- The title has a professional cover that matches genre expectations.
- The book's blurb on retailer pages is optimized to hook and convert readers.
- *Optional:* The book features editorial reviews or accolades from well-known publications or influencers.

215

Tip 4: Be flexible with your promotion dates

When applying for a Featured Deal, you can indicate whether you're flexible with your chosen discount dates. Obviously, indicating your flexibility will increase your chances of getting that deal.

Do note, however, that BookBub only schedules Featured Deals up to thirty days in advance. So if you apply for a flexible-dates Deal, make sure you're ready to drop your price across all retailers if you're accepted.

Tip 5: Keep submitting (and download our free BookBub submissions calendar)

Even if you get all of the above right and BookBub's editors think your book would make for a great deal, they might end up declining it because *other* even more attractive deals were submitted at the same time.

In other words, your chances of getting that coveted Deal also depend on the competition. And the level of competition depends on timing.

What's the solution? Keep submitting! BookBub allows you to resubmit a book every thirty days. So if you have a big list of books and you *really* want to get a deal, you can maximize your chances of landing one by continuously submitting every book you have on a thirty-day rolling basis.

Now, if a Deal is accepted, remember that BookBub won't feature the same indie author for another thirty days and the same book for another six months. So keeping track of when you can and cannot submit each book can quickly become a headache ... which is why I'm providing you with a free BookBub submissions calendar.[42]

Tip 6: Try different price points (including free)

One of the company's main tips for authors is to *keep trying*. But of course, receiving constant rejection notifications can become a bit frustrating. So the following three tips will explore what you can *change* in your resubmissions to augment your chances of getting accepted.

The first thing to try changing is the price point. BookBub's goal is to offer the best deals possible to their audience. So the lower you can go in price, the higher your chances of being accepted.

Furthermore, if you've been trying to get a $0.99 Deal for months without success, try applying for a free one instead!

Tip 7: Go wide

If your book is in Kindle Unlimited, I have some bad news for you: it'll be much, much harder to land a Featured Deal. Here's why, in BookBub's own terms:

> "When members sign up for BookBub, they opt into the retailers they want to see deals for. So if a book is available on all the major retailers—Amazon, Barnes & Noble, Apple Books, Google Play, Kobo—more of our readers would be able to snatch it up, which makes the book more appealing to our editors. Between two books with equally competitive platforms and deal prices, the editors will always choose the book available on more retailers."

At Reedsy, we personally know authors who submitted KU books to BookBub more than fifty times without ever getting accepted. One of them, Craig Martelle, finally took one of his books wide and managed to land a Featured Deal with it (albeit an international one). In his own words:[43]

> "It took me 69 tries to break the Featured Deal curse. I took a book wide so I could put it into a StoryBundle (if you ever get a chance to join a StoryBundle, I highly recommend it). Since it was wide, I applied and got an international BookBub first shot once it was wide. The book only had 35 reviews or so. After running it, I waited 30 days and then applied for US only and was then awarded with a US only feature."

Tip 8: Submit for international Deals first

When applying for a Deal, most authors either go for the full, worldwide deals, or at least US-only ones. These are the most expensive, but also the most rewarding in terms of sales and ranking boosts. But they are also harder to get. So if all your attempts at landing a global or US deal are failing, try for an international-only one. Even though they're less powerful, they can be great for boosting your international reach and presence on non-Amazon retailers.

More importantly, there's anecdotal evidence that once you get a Featured Deal, it's easier to get another one. So going for free international Deals is a way to get your foot in the door. And once that door is open, it might lead to paid worldwide or US-only Deals.

Tip 9: If everything else fails ... rebrand!

If everything above is failing, then there's probably something wrong with your book. Maybe BookBub editors don't think it fits into one of their categories. Or maybe they think the cover doesn't match the genre.

This can often be the case for books published more than three or four years ago. Genre expectations regarding covers can change quite drastically over time, so if you can't get a Featured Deal for your old books, consider rebranding them. Not only will that boost your chances of getting a Deal, but it'll also most likely boost your sales.

How to make the most of a Bookbub Featured Deal

Hurrah! Thanks to these tips, you managed to land a Featured Deal! First off, take a moment to congratulate yourself and celebrate—it's a big deal. But right after that, start planning your promo period to make the most of the Deal. Here are a few things to consider:

1. Don't discount your other books in the series

This is a common mistake for BookBub Featured Deal first timers. You want to encourage readers finding your book through the Deal to buy your other books, so you discount those as well.

But it's important to understand that BookBub readers are *deal seekers*. If they see that your other books in the series are $0.99 as well, they'll just buy them all. Great, right?

Well, not really. Because while you might be making more profit right now, you're effectively losing all the *full-price sales* you would have made when these readers finished reading your discounted book and decided to buy your other ones at full price.

2. Run the promo over a longer period

Almost everyone who has run a Featured Deal is unanimous about this: you'll get better results if you keep your discount for a longer period than the minimum days required by the service. The reason is that Amazon's algorithms largely reward *plateaus* over *spikes*.

If you raise your price right after the BookBub Deal, your sales will abruptly stop. If you keep the discount, they'll still take a dip, but it won't be as bad, which will help you maintain a high rank on Best Seller lists and trigger Amazon to take over the marketing for you.

If you're in Kindle Unlimited *and* manage to get a Featured Deal (congrats, you're a unicorn), then running the discount for longer is all the more important to make sure you climb the Popularity list and trigger a subsequent wave of page reads.

3. To stack or not to stack?

The practice of "stacking" ads is that of buying several placements on other book promotion newsletters on top of the BookBub Feature. The goal here is still the same: achieving a plateau, or an upward trend, rather than a spike.

There has been a lot of discussion in the author community on ad stacking around Featured Deals, and the consensus seems to be that:

- Ad stacking can work for paid Featured Deals.
- Ad stacking is a waste of money for free Deals.

The reason stacking can be a waste of money for free Deals is that free readers will often sign up to *as many promo sites* as possible to receive free book alerts. So by advertising your free book on several sites and newsletters, you're effectively paying more to reach the same readers.

Now, while stacking promo newsletter ads might be a waste of money, this doesn't mean you shouldn't run ads *on your own*. Facebook, Amazon, and BookBub self-serve ads will earn you a lot more sales or downloads if your book is discounted or free—if you know how to play your cards right. And that's what the next section of this book is all about!

VIII

Advertising Platforms

Dropping your book's price is not going to magically increase the number of readers who come across it. For that, you need to promote your discount. And while you can achieve that in many ways—price promotions, newsletter swaps—few are as effective as the "golden triangle" of advertising: Amazon ads, Facebook ads, and BookBub CPM/CPC ads.

38

Read through mathematics

Before we venture into each advertising platform, I have some bad news: we'll have to do a bit of math and go more in depth into read through—a concept I introduced in Chapter 8.

Read through is not only useful to understand where and when your readers are getting tired of your series; it's also a metric that can completely change the way you approach advertising.

Let's start with a simple example: You've published a great series and are just starting to play with Amazon ads. You're advertising the first book, which you've priced at an entry level of $0.99. You're getting lots of sales at an Advertising Cost of Sales (ACoS) of 50 percent, which means that every $0.99 sale you make as a result of these campaigns only costs you $0.50.

This sounds great, but the problem is that your royalty on the book is only 35 percent. So every sale earns you $0.35—not $0.99—and costs you $0.99. Naturally, you think, *I'm losing money here!* and kill the campaign.

What have you missed? Read through. You've paid to get readers to buy the first book, but a percentage of those readers will naturally go on to buy book two. If your second book is priced at, say, $2.99, and you have a read through of 50 percent:

```
Cost per sale = $0.50
Earnings per sale = $0.35 + (50% × 70% × $2.99) = $1.40
```

You just killed a campaign that was actually making *almost three times* what you were spending, with a Return on Investment (ROI) of:

```
1.4 ÷ 0.5 = 280%
```

Calculating the real ROI on your series advertising

So how do you calculate your real ROI on a long series? Well, the first step is to estimate your read through for all the books in the series, using the method outlined in Chapter 8.

Once you have that, you determine what I like to call the "lifetime value of a sale of book one" in that series. This is the average total earnings a sale of book one generates for you, including estimated read through sales.

Feeling lost? Don't worry, here's a practical example. Let's say you have a ten-book series with:

- Book one priced at $0.99
- Book two priced at $2.99, with a read through from book one to book two of 60 percent
- Book three priced at $4.99, with a read through from book one to book three of 50 percent
- Books four through ten priced at $4.99, all with a read through from book one of 45 percent

If you manage to sell one copy of book one, then the lifetime value of that sale would be:

$$(35\% \times \$0.99) + (\mathbf{60\%} \times 70\% \times \$2.99) + (\mathbf{50\%} \times 70\% \times \$4.99) + 7 \times (\mathbf{45\%} \times 70\% \times \$4.99)$$

I've put the Amazon royalty percentages in *italics* and the read through percentages in **bold**.

What does this mean? Effectively, you can afford to spend as much as fourteen dollars on advertising to generate a sale of book one. In time, and on average, you'll make that amount back.

So if you're running Facebook ads at a cost per click of $0.40 (that's quite high) and one in twenty clickers ends up buying your book (you can estimate that through Amazon Affiliate tracking, which we'll tackle in the next chapter), you could be tempted to stop the campaign. *But* that campaign is actually generating sales at a cost of:

```
$0.40 × 20 = $8
```

And guess what: That cost is less than half of what you'll eventually make back on each sale.

Not all readers are created equal

Now, if this example was eye-opening for you, that's great! But don't rush in and reactivate all the Amazon, Facebook, and BookBub campaigns you'd stopped because you thought you were losing money on them.

There are two reasons you should be cautious. The first one is obvious: the key term in "lifetime value of a sale of book one" is "lifetime." In our example above, you're spending eight dollars on Facebook ads to generate one sale of book one. But you're not going to get those eight dollars back immediately! You'll only get that return when readers make their way to book six.

Incorporating read through in your ROI calculations is important, but it can also rapidly dry up your funds. Only spend what you can afford, and keep refining your ads to drive down these costs per click and per sale.

The second reason for caution is more complex: not all readers are created equal. Let's compare John and Edward. John has picked up your first book because it was recommended by his wife, a super fan of your series. Edward has bought your first book because it was priced at $0.99 for a time and advertised on Facebook.

What is the likelihood of John reading book one and then buying all the following ones? Pretty high, right? After all, his wife can't stop raving to him about your books ...

Now, is Edward just as likely to do the same? Probably not. That's what I mean by "not all readers are created equal." Read through will depend greatly on *how the reader discovered your book.*

And unfortunately, you have no way of knowing that. In an ideal advertiser's world, you would know, for each marketing avenue:

· The cost of generating a sale through that avenue
· The average read through of readers coming from that avenue

In the publishing world, you have none of that. You can only guesstimate the *overall* cost of sale and read through numbers across *all avenues.* So while you should definitely use these estimates in your ROI calculations, you should also do so with caution.

By understanding the lifetime value of your readers, you'll start to get a picture of why it's so important to consider the series potential of any book you're writing. So long as your books keep enthralling your fans, you can keep benefitting from the investment you made in advertising your first book. Your readers get more of what they want (your fantastic books), and you get what you need (royalties).

39

Affiliates and tracking conversion

The main issue I have—as a marketer—with Amazon and other big book retailers is the lack of data and transparency. You're supposed to market your books (i.e., bring customers to them), but they won't tell you:

· Where your paying readers are coming from (referrer data)
· Which percentage of readers clicking on your book end up buying it (conversion data)

In other words, they won't tell you how you're doing. This turns the subtle science of digital marketing into, well, guesswork.

Breaking and entering into Amazon's data bank

So it's no wonder that someone quickly found a work-around to access some of Amazon's priceless data. It's the Amazon Associates Program, and it has one great pro and one great con:

· Pro: on top of giving you access to data, it can make you a small stream of additional money.
· Con: in many cases, it's technically a violation of Amazon's terms of service.

How does it work?

It's simple. You simply register for Amazon Associates,[44] Amazon's affiliate program. It's free, and you can sign in through an existing Amazon account.

Once accepted, you'll be able to generate special URLs for any Amazon item (like an e-book). When Amazon customers purchase an item through that URL, Amazon tracks it, *reports it to you*, and pays you a small referral fee.

For example, let's say you're trying to estimate the conversion of book one in your series. Your first step will be to generate an affiliate link for your book. Go to the Product Linking section of your affiliate dashboard and search for your book name or ASIN.

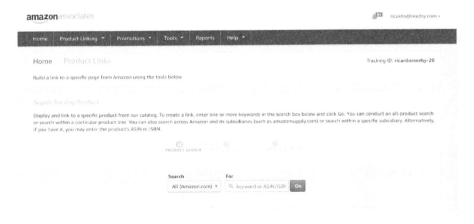

Then click on the little arrow next to "Get link" and grab the shortened Amzn.to link.

Use that link in your ads and get a good number of clicks on it. After a few days, check the Reports section in your affiliate dashboard.

Product Title	Product Link Clicks	Product Link Conversion	Ordered Through Product Links	All Other Items Ordered	Total Items Ordered
	1,284	5.30%	68	0	68
	721	6.80%	49	0	49
	1,673	1.43%	24	0	24
	1,309	0.61%	8	0	8
	13	15.38%	2	0	2
	443	0.45%	2	0	2

Ta-da! You'll be able to view the conversion performance of all your links.

"But isn't this strictly forbidden by Amazon?"

Yes and no. You're more than welcome (actually encouraged) by Amazon to set up an Amazon Associates account, generate affiliate links for your books, and promote your books using those links.

According to Amazon's Terms of Use, however, you should always disclose the fact you're an affiliate, and more importantly, you should never run *advertisements* with those links.

So if you post that affiliate link on your Facebook Page? You're fine.

If you boost that post (i.e., turn it into an ad), you're technically breaching Amazon's Terms of Use.

Now, what happens if you use affiliate codes in ads and get caught? In my case (because it's happened to me), and in the few other cases I've heard about, the Amazon Associates account was closed. The only things I lost were affiliate income and data—but I didn't see a negative impact on ranks, reviews, or anything really important.

All this is to say: it's relatively safe to use affiliate links in ads, and also to use this system to monitor conversion data. I wouldn't run them continuously, but instead test for a few weeks to estimate your conversion and then keep running ads without the affiliate link.

```
Pro tip: if you want to keep track of two different marketing
channels (e.g., Facebook Ads and BookBub Ads) you can do so
within the same Associates account by setting up two different
tracking codes.
```

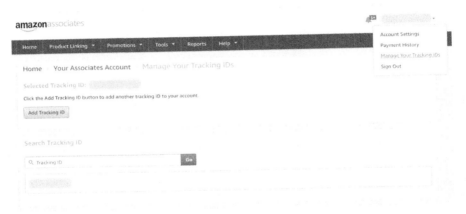

Now, it's likely that Amazon will eventually crack down more severely on the use of affiliate links in ads, or even pass an agreement with Facebook so that advertisers can't use them. (I'm starting to see some warnings like this on the Facebook advertising platform.) If that happens, you can send your ads to an intermediary landing page (e.g., on your website) where you have the affiliate links to your book on Amazon. That's allowed, and while the added step in the process will lose you some sales, the data you'll gather will be worth it.

Conversion tracking on wide retailers

The cool thing is that this method for tracking conversion (and earning some pocket money) works on the other major retailers as well:

- Apple Books and Google Play offer an affiliate program managed through Partnerize, which works well and is even more intuitive than the Amazon one. Just search for "Apple Books affiliate" or "Google Play affiliate" to find them.
- Kobo eBooks also has an affiliate program you can sign up for via Rakuten Advertising. It's extremely confusing, though.

For all of these, it's the same idea: you create affiliate links to your books and plug them into your different marketing channels. And the best part about Apple, Google, and Kobo affiliate programs is that they allow you to use their links in ads—so you can do so safely without worrying about your affiliate account getting suspended.

Do I really need to do this?

No. Using affiliate tracking is a pretty advanced method to estimate the conversion of your book's landing pages. It's important to know about it because it's the closest thing to "real data" you can get from the retailers, but it's only valuable to authors running Facebook and BookBub ads.

40

Amazon vs. Facebook vs. BookBub

Before we get into the nitty-gritty of running ads on these different platforms, it's worth taking a big-picture look at each one and comparing their strengths and weaknesses. You probably won't have the time and energy to run ads on all three, so you need to understand which works best in which situation, as well as the skills and mindset each requires, in order to choose the *one* you'll get started on and test.

Remember my advice from the very first chapters: you can't test everything at the same time! The goal of this chapter is to help you make an informed decision on which advertising platform to test first. The following chapters offer you some in-depth information on the mechanics of each, as well as tips to set up your first (successful) ads.

Amazon ads: A slow drip for all price points

Prime real estate

I like to start with the advertising platform owned by the world's biggest book retailer, because, well, it's owned by the world's biggest book retailer. And that's the main thing that sets it apart from Facebook and BookBub: the ads you run on Amazon show up *directly on Amazon*, a place where, you know, people actually buy books. You're reaching readers when they're looking for their next read—not when they're watching cute puppies dance.

Even better, Amazon lets you target specific keywords—like book titles or author names—so by using the right keywords and bids, you can get your book to show up on the product pages of the most famous books in your genre, or even in search results for people who search for these famous books.

Accurate sales reporting

The great advantage Amazon Advertising has over Facebook or BookBub is that it tells you exactly how many books your ads have sold.

In fact, Amazon Advertising is the only channel where you can accurately track your results down to the very sale of the book. For other ads, you have to use affiliate codes (as discussed in the previous chapter) to track your sales, and then create a spreadsheet to reconcile everything. With Amazon ads, you have all the info in the dashboard and can easily visualize which campaigns and keywords are making you, or costing you, money.

A cost-per-click model

This is another important characteristic of Amazon Advertising: you are only charged when people (readers) *click* on your ads. So say, for example, that you're targeting "Harry Potter." Not only would your book show up in search results for "Harry Potter," you wouldn't have to pay a cent until someone clicks on your book.

This means you can get a lot of prime real estate and spread your brand for free, at least until someone clicks on and checks out your book.

A platform for higher price points

Perhaps the best benefit of Amazon Advertising is that it is relatively easy (at least compared to the other two platforms) to get a positive return on investment even on higher-priced books. This has to do with the fact that the ads show up on Amazon, where people are already predisposed to spend money—and usually more than a couple of dollars.

That's great for pushing print books as well as nonfiction e-books (which tend to be priced a bit higher than fiction).

A nightmare to scale

"Wait, if Amazon Advertising is so great, why isn't everyone spending tons of money on it?" Well, that's because Amazon Advertising makes it pretty difficult to spend a lot of money. While it's relatively easy to get a positive return on investment (ROI) with Amazon ads, it's very hard to *scale* your efforts and get Amazon to spend your whole budget—and generate a ton of sales. Here's an anonymized example from a client's dashboard:

As you can see, though I set up a *daily budget* of $500 on the first campaign, Amazon spent under fifteen dollars per day on it. (The figures are for the last seven days.) The hard part isn't getting sales and making a profit; it's replicating and scaling that success.

Because of this, Amazon Advertising is known as the best platform to achieve a *constant but small drip of sales*, with a positive ROI. That is in stark contrast to Facebook and BookBub, where it's much harder to achieve a positive ROI, but a lot easier to get a big boost in sales—you just have to spend more.

Complexity level: Medium

Amazon as a company has been investing a lot of resources into developing their advertising solution and becoming a strong competitor to Google and Facebook. That said, they are years behind those platforms in that area, and it shows—just look at the Amazon Advertising dashboard.

Setting up an ad is relatively easy. You just select the product to advertise, your budget, a targeting method (automatic or keywords), and a bid. The fact that you don't have to create an ad image or come up with a lot of ad copy makes the whole process a lot easier, too.

The problem, though, comes when you want to monitor and optimize your ads. The advertising dashboard isn't particularly intuitive and lacks some essential features like cross-campaign editing or simple A/B testing for advertising copy. Overall, Amazon ads are a pain to monitor and update—which is why some automated optimization tools like Prestozon are having so much success.

BookBub ads: A simple platform to boost cheap and free books

"Wait, didn't you already write a whole chapter about BookBub?" Yes. But that chapter was about BookBub *Featured Deals*—which are manually curated by BookBub's editorial team and very hard to obtain. BookBub *ads* are a different feature: it's their self-serve advertising platform where you buy ad placement in BookBub's newsletters. We call those "BookBub self-serve ads" or "BookBub CPM/CPC ads" (since you pay for those on a CPM or CPC basis).

```
CPM: cost per thousand impressions
CPC: cost per click
```

The interesting thing is that BookBub self-serve ads are the opposite of Amazon ads: they're all about images (which you need to create), they don't work well for full-price books, they're tough to master, and they're very easy to scale.

Prime real estate ... for cheap and free books

BookBub self-serve ads are mostly served at the bottom of BookBub's daily newsletters announcing the Featured Deals. As such, they're a great way to buy some prime real estate in one of the most authoritative places when it comes to cheap and free books.

That said, if your book is *not* discounted or free, then you'll probably find BookBub ads a lot less effective—after all, readers subscribe to BookBub and open their newsletters purely because they are seeking *deals*. If you don't have one to offer them, they might very well snub you.

Complexity level: Easy

BookBub Ads is the most recent advertising platform of the three, and as such it's also the easiest one to navigate. The whole ad creation interface fits on one page and is pretty intuitive.

You just have to name your ad, upload or create your ad image, and select targeting, budget, and bid, and you're good to go. That said, you will have to spend quite a lot of time creating ad image variations to test, and testing audiences as well.

Testing, testing, and more testing

This is the main pain point and barrier to entry when it comes to BookBub ads: it takes *a lot* of testing to find a winning image/targeting combination.

If you're a bit savvy, and somewhat lucky, you could end up with a profitable advertising campaign on Facebook or Amazon on your first try—but that's extremely unlikely for BookBub. Instead, you'll have to invest quite a bit of time (and money) into methodical testing, which can quickly become discouraging.

That said, if you stick to it and find those winning combinations, then you're golden! BookBub ads are super easy to scale. You just have to feed BookBub more money and let them turn it into book sales—until you exhaust your audiences, of course.

Facebook ads: A complex Swiss Army knife

Mixed real estate

As opposed to Amazon and BookBub, Facebook is *not* focused on books. This is not to mean that you can't reach book lovers through Facebook ads, but you won't reach them at a time when they're actively looking for books.

Your ad might show in the feed right below the cutest kitten video ever, and receive next to no attention as a result. Or it might interrupt someone browsing through their Instagram stories and annoy them. *Or it might show up at exactly the right time for a reader who was just thinking about grabbing their next read.*

In short: you don't know. Facebook is much more of a "spray and pray" platform than BookBub and Amazon, which are focused on readers. But because Facebook has built such a strong advertising platform with machine learning algorithms that can swiftly identify who is most likely to click on your ads, it's relatively easy to get *a lot of clicks* on them at a pretty low cost per click (think $0.10–$0.20).

Cheap clicks, expensive sales

The great thing with clicks is that they bring readers to your retailer product page. The bad thing is that once these readers are there, you have no idea what they do next. While Amazon Advertising gives you clear visibility down to the *sale*, you don't have that with Facebook or BookBub. You know how many clicks you get and the cost per click, but there is no exact way to know *how* many readers who click on the ad end up buying the book—unless you use Amazon Associates tracking.

What I've found from running Facebook ads for dozens of different authors (in as many different genres), is that conversion rates from Facebook ads on Amazon generally range from 0.5 percent to 10 percent. In practice, this means that for every one thousand clicks you get on Facebook ads, you'd sell between five and one hundred books.

I know that's a broad range, but it's to show that you can run ads on Amazon that get you a ton of clicks—and next to no sales. In fact, it's quite common, especially on higher-priced books. *But the opposite is quite common as well, so the only way to know is to test them.*

I'll say this, though: I've found Facebook ads to be most effective at low price points (free or $0.99), which makes sense if you remember that, again, you're reaching an audience not actively looking to buy a book, so you need a compelling offer for them to leave the puppy videos.

Lead ads, carousel ads, video ads ...

The best thing about Facebook is the incredible range of test factors. If simple single-static-image ads don't work, you can try video ads instead. Or you can group both into a dynamic ad.

If you're wide and you want to boost your sales on non-Amazon retailers, you can easily target Kobo, Apple Books, and Google Play readers through Facebook.

If sending readers straight to retailers doesn't work, you can try list-building ads with a reader magnet on BookFunnel instead.

If you have a series, you can run carousel or collection ads to advertise all of your books in the series at once.

You get the gist: the possibilities on Facebook are infinite, and once you start mastering this Swiss Army knife, you can use it for many more things than just sending readers to your first-in-series on Amazon.

Complexity level: Hard

Remember the first time you held a Swiss Army knife? I bet you didn't know where to begin. Well, it's easy to get the same feeling on Facebook Ads.

It's not that the platform is badly designed or unintuitive; it's just that it has *so many features* that it's easy to get lost or miss something crucial.

Moreover, while Amazon ads require next to no effort to set up (because you can't really customize them), Facebook ads will require a headline, a short description, and hook copy above the image—all of which you need to come up with and test, on top of the image itself.

Don't get scared, though: once you get the hang of it, setting up an ad on Facebook is quick, and the results are nearly immediate.

Personally, Facebook is my favorite advertising platform, and the one where I tend to get the best results—but I know countless authors who much prefer Amazon or BookBub ads. My goal throughout this chapter was to give you a brief overview of how each of these three platforms works so you can make a decision on *which to test first.*

You won't have the time nor the energy to run ads everywhere—and more importantly, you probably won't be good at all three. So pick the one you think has the most potential to be successful for you and your books, and read the upcoming chapters dedicated to it. For example, if you think BookBub ads are a safe bet, skip the Amazon ads section and focus your time on learning about and perfecting BookBub ads.

41

Amazon Advertising I: Setting up your first campaign

It's finally time to get into the nitty-gritty of each of the three advertising platforms, starting with Amazon. Of course, each platform is complex enough to warrant a whole book, so I won't be able to go into all the details here. Instead, I'll teach you the basics and then point you in the right direction to learn more.

All in all, my aim in these chapters is to cover two basic but crucial lessons:

1. How to create your first advertising campaign
2. How to monitor and optimize your campaigns, with the goal of achieving a positive return on investment

Without further ado, let's get started!

The first step is to go to your KDP Bookshelf and click on "Promote & Advertise" next to your title, then select the country store in which you want to advertise. What this will do is effectively create an Amazon Advertising account for you in the country you selected—which you'll then have to supplement with your billing and payment information.

Once you're finished, you'll see that Amazon offers you two different ad options: Sponsored Product and Product Display. There will be links in the endnotes to learn more about each of them, but the vast majority of authors I know get their best results with Sponsored Product ads, so I suggest you start there. As such, I only cover Sponsored Product ads in this chapter.

Advertised products and budget

The next step is to select the book(s) and format(s) (e-book, paperback) you want to advertise. Now, since July 1, 2020, Amazon Advertising only reports sales for the formats you selected in each campaign. Why is this important? I'll illustrate it with an example. Let's say you have only one book out, in both e-book and paperback:

- If you add *only* the e-book to your campaign, readers clicking on your ad will be taken straight to the e-book page. But some of them might buy it as a paperback. However, these paperback sales *won't* be reported on your Amazon Advertising dashboard.
- The same logic applies if you add *only* the paperback to your advertising campaign: your ads will be for the paperback only, and e-book sales generated by the ads won't be reported in the dashboard.
- If you add both the e-book and paperback to your campaign, Amazon will report sales for both formats, *but* will randomly show either the e-book ad or the paperback ad to shoppers. You won't have any control over which format gets shown predominantly in the ad.

What does this mean, practically? Well, if 90 percent of your sales come from one format, then you're better off advertising *that format* only—you won't know if your ads generate sales of the other format, but it's unlikely enough for you to not care. If your sales are balanced across formats, then you'll probably want to include all the formats in your campaigns; otherwise it'll be impossible for you to know which are profitable.

Once you've selected the books and formats you want to advertise, you'll have to set a daily budget for the campaign. I suggest you start at five to ten dollars. Chances are, you'll only be spending a small portion of that budget

HOW TO MARKET A BOOK

...

Targeting

Next comes the targeting. Amazon Advertising gives you two options for targeting:

- Automatic targeting: you let Amazon choose where they feature your book.
- Manual targeting: you set keywords or categories you'd like to target.

I recommend testing both (in separate campaigns), but I've found that manual targeting works better *unless* your book is in a nonfiction niche, has impeccable metadata, and has clean Also Boughts.

In any case, setting an autotargeting campaign is always a good idea. Amazon might autofind keywords that you hadn't thought about on your own—and you'll be able to view those by running "search term reports."

With the manual option, the trick is to add a lot of *relevant* keywords. Manual keyword selection is the only intricate part of using Amazon ads, so I'll cover it in more detail in the next chapter. Meanwhile, I recommend you find twenty authors in your genre you want to target and add their names and the titles of all their books (in your genre) as keywords. It's a good place to start.

Setting a bid

The last step before designing the ad is setting a bid. This is the amount you're ready to pay for a click on your ad. As reckless as it sounds, I suggest you bid high ($0.50 or so). This will ensure that your ads start serving quickly and gather impressions and clicks. These clicks might cost you more, but that's something you can fine-tune later: in the beginning what's important is to test keywords quickly.

Advertising copy

The great thing about Amazon Advertising is that you won't spend hours (or days) creating and split testing your ad images. Amazon simply uses your cover. Just note that certain covers (e.g., ones suggesting sexual behavior) may make a book ineligible for Amazon ads. You can read Amazon Advertising's official "Creative Acceptance Policies" to learn more.[45]

So the only thing you get to play with is the copy, which is limited to 150 characters. I've found that ad copy works best when it focuses on just one of the following:

- An excerpt from a glowing review: *"[Author name] has done it again: an engrossing read that will keep you turning the pages" —Kirkus Reviews*
- Plot-based copy: *Steven didn't suspect that pursuing her could destroy his career. Emma didn't realize what trusting him would cost her.*
- Social validation: *Downloaded 100,000 times already, this first book in the [Name of Your Series] series will get you hooked.*
- Comp authors or titles: *Fans of Scout Finch (*To Kill A Mockingbird*) and Jo March (*Little Women*) will treasure Louisa May "Wildflower" McAllister in this well-loved novel.*

```
Note: In certain Amazon country stores (e.g., Amazon.ca or
Amazon.uk.), you don't get the option to add customized copy.
Similarly, if you run campaigns that advertise more than one
product or format, you won't be able to use custom copy. This
will make your job even easier, even if your ads are slightly
less catchy as a result.
```

I suggest you look up the books you want to target on Amazon and scroll down to the "Sponsored products related to this item." (If you can't see them, deactivate your ad blocker.) Take inspiration from the copy used by other advertisers.

That's it—you have your first ad! Once you publish it, it'll go into "review" and should be accepted by Amazon within twenty-four hours (provided you've followed their guidelines). Your job doesn't end here, though. You'll have to monitor your campaign, find more keywords to target, and once you find something that works, try to scale it.

42

Amazon Advertising II: Finding more keywords

I've said it already, but I'll say it again: the *real* challenge with Amazon ads is not return on investment; it's *scalability*.

It's easy enough to find keywords that yield a super-low Advertising Cost of Sale (ACoS) and much trickier to find a keyword that brings you *a lot* of sales. In other words, it's hard to get Amazon to spend your advertising budget.

This is why I suggested bidding high when you first test a keyword. If you don't, it can take weeks before you get enough impressions on that keyword to know whether it's worth it.

Now, where most authors go wrong with Amazon ads is that they only include a dozen keywords in their campaign. Even if one of these works, it'll only bring a few sales per month—which is not going to move the needle.

You need to test *hundreds* of keywords and find at least fifty that work for you. If you have fifty keywords bringing you two or three sales every week, then you'll be cooking with gas!

HOW TO MARKET A BOOK

Finding keywords

The great thing about Amazon Advertising is that you only pay when people click on your ad. So you can afford to go a bit broad with your keyword targeting: if a keyword is not relevant, people won't click on your ad, so you won't pay anyway. It's not like Facebook ads, where sloppy targeting can cost you a lot of money.

The main types of keywords you want to target are:

· Book titles in your genre
· Author names in your genre
· Genres and subgenres

I suggest you build a spreadsheet with these three columns, and fill it with two hundred keywords or so.

Author names	Book titles	Other keywords
ann swinfen	the eller's tale	italian renaissance
kevin ashman	medieval blood of the cross	italian renaissance art
jennifer siddoway	the highlander's secret	italian renaissance women in the renaissance
jennifer anne davis	the key	italian renaissance books
colin falconer	silk road	italian renaissance novel
emma prince	her wild highlander	medieval fiction
claire delacroix	the crusader's bride	medieval fiction kindle
griff hosker	baron's war	medieval fiction books
alice coldbreath	his forsaken bride	medieval fiction novels
james carroll	the cloister	gothic fiction
ann swinfen	sparknotes	gothic fiction books
kevin ashman	anne rice vampire chronicles	middle ages
jennifer siddoway	anne rice sleeping beauty trilogy	middle ages history
jennifer anne davis	anne rice collection	middle ages historical fiction
jh plumb	anne rice sleeping beauty trilogy	middle ages italy
robin maxwell	anne rice christ the lord	middle ages romance
ada palmer	anne rice mayfair witches	middle ages boxset
david young kim	anne rice witching hour	middle ages series
c de melo	anne rice blood communion	verona
stephanie storey	anne rice exit to eden	verona italy
anne rice	anne rice interview with a vampire	renaissance fiction
jean plaidy	anne rice queen of the damned	italian historical fiction
judith lennox	anne rice ramses the damned the passion of cleopatra	renaissance historical fiction
marina fiorato	anne rice the mummy	renaissance

Example of an Amazon Advertising keyword research spreadsheet

246

Author names

Amazon makes it easy to find the names of your comp authors (even ones you didn't suspect). If you go to your Amazon Author Central page, you'll see a Customers Also Bought Items By section in the sidebar.

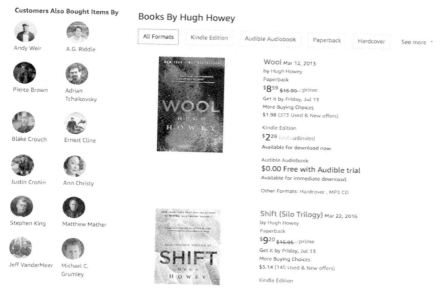

Hugh Howey's Amazon Author Central page

These work like the Also Boughts on a particular book's page. Add all these names to the "author names" column of your spreadsheet. Then go into each of these authors' pages and repeat the operation. This should get you a good fifty author names.

Book titles

You could apply the same technique to titles using the Also Boughts, but considering books often have more than fifty Also Boughts, copying and pasting them all can take you a full day. Thankfully, there's a great tool that can make this process go a lot faster: Publisher Rocket.[46] It's not a free tool, but if you're going to invest money in Amazon ads, you might as well invest a little bit extra to buy the tool: it'll save you both time and money in the long run.

Here's how it works: You just plug in a keyword (e.g., an author name or book title), and Publisher Rocket returns a huge list of related keywords (Also Boughts, products that show in the search results for your keyword, etc.). You can filter to remove the keywords that are not 100 percent relevant, and then export the list. Repeat this operation for two or three keywords, and this should add another two hundred keywords to your spreadsheet.

Genres and subgenres

It's equally important to target genre keywords, as this will allow your book to appear in the search results for these genres, and on the category pages.

Now, I can't find a hack for quickly uncovering lots of keywords related to your genre or subgenre—short of using Publisher Rocket—but using Amazon's autocomplete in the search bar is a good method. For example, if you write historical romance:

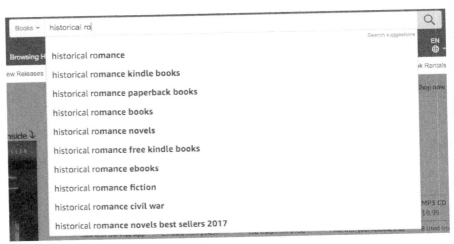

Copy all these results into your spreadsheet (except the ones that don't make sense, like "paperback" or "free"), and repeat the operation for any subgenres you can think of (e.g., "Victorian romance," "regency," etc.).

248

Separating the wheat from the chaff

Once you have a solid list of at least two hundred keywords, add all of those to a brand-new Amazon Advertising campaign. Again, bid relatively high: the goal here is to test the keywords, and you'll only pay if you get a click.

Leave that campaign running until it's gathered a good number of clicks (at least fifty) and then go in and take a look at how each keyword has performed. You should monitor your campaigns on a weekly basis, but I don't recommend doing it more often than that. Amazon ads are *slow* compared to Facebook or BookBub ads: it takes time for the campaigns to start gathering impressions and clicks, so monitoring often can lead to making hasty decisions based on incomplete data.

"What kinds of decisions?" you may ask. Well, that's for the next chapter.

43

Amazon Advertising III: Monitoring and optimizing

Monitoring Amazon ads is one of the things I enjoy the least in the world of advertising. The dashboard is horrible, and it lacks a bunch of basic functions that would make all our lives easier.

But we make do with what we have, and the silver lining is that you don't need to monitor your Amazon ads that often. I do it once a week and follow a simple but strategic method I'll outline below.

Taking care of your CTR

I mentioned that one of the great things about Amazon ads is that you only pay per click. So even if you run ads that get a lot of *impressions* (i.e., are seen by a lot of readers) but don't get any clicks, you don't have to pay anything.

That's 100 percent true, but it doesn't mean you shouldn't care if your ads fall into that category. See, if Amazon notices that your campaign doesn't generate clicks, it'll be a lot less inclined to serve it—because it's not making much money from it.

So even if it doesn't directly impact your revenue, the *click-through rate* (or CTR) is one of the most important metrics to monitor and take good care of in your Amazon advertising campaigns. What's the CTR? It's simply the ratio of clicks divided by impressions. A low CTR is the ultimate indicator (to both you and Amazon) that the readers you're trying to reach with your ads don't care about your book.

"*So what's a good CTR?*" Excellent question. It varies a lot by genre and by type of campaign, but I personally try to shoot for more than 0.2 percent on Sponsored Product campaigns. So the first thing I do when I check my campaigns is filter the keyword list by "CTR < 0.2 percent." This immediately identifies which keywords are hurting the campaign's overall CTR and might ultimately hinder Amazon from further serving my campaign.

I regularly go in and cull any keywords that meet *all* these criteria:

- Have a CTR below 0.2 percent
- Have received at least two hundred impressions
- Haven't produced any sales

Of course, these thresholds aren't set in stone. Even if a keyword has driven a sale or two, if its CTR is extremely low I may very well pause it. And I might leave some keywords with a low CTR for branding purposes.

The main takeaways are that CTR is important and that you should regularly monitor the CTR of your keywords to weed out underperforming ones.

The ACoS controversy

If you've used, or even just read about, Amazon Advertising before, then I'm sure you'll have come across this metric: the ACoS, or "Advertising Cost of Sale." So what does it mean, exactly, and how important is it?

Despite the controversy surrounding it, the ACoS is a pretty simple metric: it's the ratio of spend (cost) divided by sales.

```
CTR = clicks divided by impressions
ACoS = cost divided by sales
```

For example, if you've spent fifteen dollars on a campaign, that campaign generated five sales of your e-book, and your e-book is priced at $2.99, the Amazon Advertising dashboard will show:

- Cost: $15
- Orders: 5
- Sales: $14.95 ($2.99 × 5)
- ACoS: 100.33% (15 ÷ $14.95)

An ACoS of 100 percent means that your campaign has generated as much money in sales as you spend on it. So in the wider world of advertising, an ACoS of 100 percent means you're breaking even.

But the thing with Amazon is that you're only earning a portion of the sales figure. If you sell five e-books at $2.99, you're not making $14.95; you're actually making 70 percent of that (if not less). Which is why you might have heard of the "70 percent rule" when it comes to the ACoS. If you earn 70 percent in royalties on e-book sales on Amazon, then any campaign (or keyword) with an ACoS *below* 70 percent is making you money.

Sadly, this 70 percent rule is far from perfect, and so is the ACoS metric. For starters, it doesn't work well with paperback ads. Royalties on paperback sales are much harder to calculate, so you'd have to figure out exactly how much money you make on a paperback sale to calculate what your ACoS should be to break even.

It gets much worse, though, if you advertise several formats (e.g., e-book and paperback) within the same campaign. In such cases, Amazon will give you the breakdown of sales and ACoS for each format, but only at the overall campaign level, not for each keyword. So say you have a keyword that has brought in one hundred dollars in sales—you won't know if those were mainly e-book or paperback sales.

Even worse, let's say you run a price promotion for a couple of weeks and drop your price to $0.99 (a price at which you earn only 35 percent in royalties). When looking at your ads' performance for the month, the ACoS metric will be completely meaningless because you'll have sales at both full price and $0.99 in there, at different royalty levels ... so it'll be impossible to work out whether the campaign was profitable by just looking at the ACoS.

Factoring in read through and Kindle Unlimited

Despite all this, Amazon advertising is the only ad platform that gives you *some* data on sales, so we shouldn't complain, right?

Well, sometimes some incomplete data is worse than none, because it can lead you to make wrong decisions. Remember the chapter on read through? Well, read through data isn't factored at all into your Amazon Advertising dashboard. If you have a long series with strong read through, an ACoS of even 200 percent might actually signal a profitable campaign or keyword, because only sales of book one are factored into the ACoS.

More importantly, while Kindle Unlimited borrows and reads are reported in the Amazon Advertising dashboard (as of July 2020), they are not factored into the ACoS.

All this contributes to making the ACoS an incomplete and unreliable metric. But it's the best thing we have, and when grouped with orders and sales numbers, it can give you a good idea of whether a keyword is performing well.

Figuring out your target ACoS or cost per order

Bearing all this in mind, the most important step in monitoring and optimizing your Amazon ads is *figuring out your target ACoS*, i.e., the ACoS at which you estimate you're breaking even. This will be your reference point when analyzing your campaigns.

How do you figure out your target ACoS? Well, you look at your historical read through performance. To make this clearer, let's look at the fictional examples of John and Jane.

```
John has a trilogy with all three books priced at $3.99, and:
- a read through to book two of 40 percent
- a read through to book three of 30 percent
```

So when John sells a copy of book one, he can expect to make:

```
70% × ($3.99 + $3.99 × 40% + $3.99 × 30%) = $4.75
```

This is the amount John can afford to spend on advertising to generate *one* sale. In Amazon Advertising terms, spending $4.75 to generate $3.99 in sales would mean an ACoS of:

```
4.75 ÷ 3.99 = 1.19
```

So John's target ACoS is 119 percent. Any campaign with an ACoS below that will make John money, and vice versa any campaign with a higher ACoS will not be profitable. Now let's look at Jane.

```
Jane has the exact same trilogy, with the exact same read
through, except her books are in Kindle Unlimited--and she gets
twice as many KU borrows as sales. Her books are 350 Kindle
Edition Normalized Pages (KENP) long, and the current KU payout
per page is $0.0042.
```

When Jane sells a copy of book one, she can expect to make $4.75 in the long term on that sale, just like John. But unlike John, what she spent on ads to generate that sale probably generated, *on average*, two KU borrows as well—which won't be visible as such in the Amazon Advertising dashboard. For her, a borrow of book one is worth:

```
$0.0042 × (350 + 350 × 40% + 350 × 30%) = $2.50
```

So these two borrows of book one are worth five dollars total to her in the long term. Which means that she can afford to spend up to $4.75 plus $5, which equals $9.75, on ads to generate just *one* sale (because that sale will likely be accompanied by two untracked KU borrows).

In terms of Amazon Advertising, it means her target ACoS is:

```
$9.75 ÷ $3.99 = 2.44, or 244%
```

Of course, you don't need to follow math to the letter (or number?), and can instead choose to be more conservative with your targets. What these two examples seek to illustrate is that most of the time, 70 percent is *not* the right target for your ACoS. You can have campaigns with a much higher ACoS that actually make you much more money. So you need to figure out which target ACoS you're *comfortable* with. And you can validate your assumptions by monitoring the evolution of your page reads (now reported in the Amazon Advertising dashboard as well).

Sometimes, though, the ACoS is just completely unusable. For example, if you advertise both your paperback and e-book in the same campaign, the "sales" figure in the dashboard and the ACoS will include both e-book and print sales, on which you earn a very different royalty level.

In such cases, it might be a better idea to use another metric: the *cost per order*. Amazon doesn't show it to you in the dashboard, but it's fairly easy to calculate: just divide the cost of the campaign by the number of orders it generated.

For example, if you know you make around three dollars on a sale of an e-book and $2.50 on the corresponding paperback, then you can set a conservative target *cost per order* of $2.50. You'll know that any campaign with a lower cost per order is most definitely making you money, regardless of the ACoS.

Monitoring and optimizing

Once you have that target metric, optimizing your ads is easy—at least *in theory*—because you know what to shoot for.

Here's how *I* personally go about it. After I've removed all the keywords that damage the campaign's CTR, I look *exclusively* at two things: my key metric (ACoS or cost per order) and clicks:

- If a keyword's key metric is below my target, I don't touch it (or slightly increase the bid to get more impressions on it).
- If a keyword has had fewer than ten to fifteen clicks, I don't touch it, either; there's not enough data to make a decision here.
- If a keyword has had more than ten to fifteen clicks and the key metric is slightly above my target, I reduce the bid.
- If a keyword has had more than ten to fifteen clicks and the key metric is way above my target, I turn it off.

Here's an example taken from an anonymized Amazon dashboard. Note that the keywords for which the ACoS shows "–" are ones that generated no sale.

Active	Keyword	▾ Clicks ⓘ	ACOS ⓘ	ACoS target: 50%
	Total: 30	283	83.30%	
		54	90.89%	⟶ Switch off
		43	44.96%	⟶ Don't touch
		34	–	⟶ Switch off
		27	–	⟶ Switch off
		22	38.71%	⟶ Slightly raise bid
		16	75.32%	⟶ Lower bid
		9	–	⟶ Don't touch

If you're wondering why my target ACoS is so low, it's because this campaign advertises a paperback, for which the author's royalties are lower than for an e-book.

Now, I'm not claiming that's how *everyone* should do it. You might not want to wait until a keyword gets ten clicks and no sales before shutting it off. Or you might not want to raise bids. That's fine—the idea here is to give you an example of a workflow to review and optimize your ads, so that you can develop your own.

Amazon Advertising resources

I mentioned earlier that the topic of Amazon Advertising is vast enough to warrant a whole book—if not a series. My goal here was to give you enough information to (1) get started and set up your first campaigns and (2) run some profitable ads. Once you get there, though, and if you determine that Amazon ads are *the marketing channel* to focus on for your books, you'll want to build up your knowledge with specialist resources created by Amazon Advertising experts.

I don't consider myself an expert on Amazon ads—I do for Facebook ads—but I know several authors who are. I've learnt a lot from their books and courses, so I couldn't feel more comfortable recommending them to you. Without further ado:

- *Mastering Amazon Ads: An Author's Guide,*[47] by Brian D. Meeks: probably the most famous book on Amazon ads, it'll teach you everything you need to know.
- *Amazon Ads Unleashed: Advanced Publishing and Marketing Strategies for Indie Authors,*[48] by Robert J. Ryan: one of the most recent guides to Amazon ads, with some more-advanced tips for optimization
- Felicia Beasley's "Going Deep with Amazon Advertising" course:[49] Felicia is one of the most knowledgeable people I know when it comes to Amazon ads—she's run the ads of several six-figure authors. Her course only periodically opens up for enrollment, so I recommend signing up

to her newsletter to get an e-mail when it does.

· Mark Dawson's "Ads for Authors" course:[50] Mark's course has a huge in-depth module on Amazon ads produced by Janet Margot, an ex-Amazon Advertising employee (in charge of Book Ads). So you get one of the creators behind Amazon Advertising for books to teach you about the platform. Not cheap, but most certainly worth it.

Note: Some of the links in the endnotes are affiliate links. However, I only ever recommend books or courses that I have read or taken and benefitted from, and that I genuinely believe are the best-available resources for any author.

44

BookBub Ads I: Your first campaign

As mentioned in the introductory chapter of this section, BookBub is by far the easiest advertising platform to get started on. The only things you'll need to set up your first campaign are some minor comp author research and some design skills.

Links and retailers

To get started, just head to partners.bookbub.com and sign up as an author. Before you do anything else, you'll want to claim your author profile and books on the site—it's free, and it's a good way to grow your following on the BookBub platform. It'll also simplify the ad setup process.

Once you have your author profile up and running, just head to BookBub Ads in the sidebar and click on "Create an ad."

As you'll see, the whole ad creation interface sits on just one page—a welcome change from platforms like Amazon and Facebook.

The first thing you'll have to decide is simple: which book you want to advertise. If you've claimed and verified your author profile, all your books will be available in a drop-down menu. When selecting one, BookBub will autofill the "links" section with the links of your book on all the different retailers.

If you haven't verified your profile yet, no worries! You can simply enter the links yourself.

Pro tip: Most people enter simple retailer links, but note that
you can enter any link there, including links to your own
website, affiliate links, or links with embedded tracking (like
ReaderLinks or Booklinker links). The only links BookBub won't
allow are those to a reader magnet page: you can't use BookBub
ads for list building.

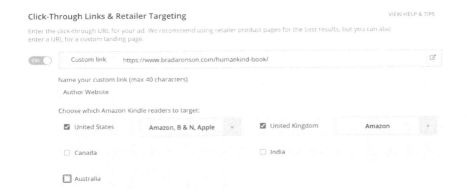

For each link, you have to specify what store and country it is aimed at.
BookBub will use the information to know which readers to show your ad to.

For example, if you fill in the Amazon US, Amazon UK, B&N, and Apple
Books US links, BookBub will show your ads to:

· US readers whom they've identified as Amazon, B&N, and/or Apple
  Books buyers
· UK readers whom they've identified as Amazon buyers

So they won't show your ads to, say, UK Apple Books buyers or Kobo
buyers. This is a great opportunity for wide authors because it allows you
to create laser-focused ads to grow sales on specific non-Amazon retailers,
something that is harder to do on Facebook and obviously impossible
through Amazon Advertising.

Since this is your first campaign, your main objective is *testing*, so I recommend you start with "Amazon US" as a testing playground. It's obviously the most competitive store to get results on, but that means that if you find something that works for that country's store, it'll work even better for other countries and retailers.

Select Reading Format
VIEW HELP & TIPS
What type of readers do you want to reach?

⦿ Ebook readers
○ Audiobook listeners

Another cool thing you can do with BookBub ads is target audiobook listeners specifically. BookBub launched an audiobook promotion service in 2019 called Chirp, so they have a solid database of audiobook listeners in every genre. Just make sure to tick the "audiobook" box when setting up the ad, and put a link to your audiobook on Chirp. This last part is not mandatory — you can also use any audiobook retailer link (Audible, Amazon, Apple Books, Kobo, etc.), however only ads pointing to a Chirp URL are eligible to show on Chirp newsletters. Other ads will still compete for impressions in regular BookBub newsletters — and BookBub does collect info from members on whether they listen to audiobooks — however that audience will be much smaller than the Chirp one.

In the rest of this chapter, I'll focus solely on e-book ads for simplicity, but most of the advice applies to audiobook ads, too.

Targeting

Once you've selected which book to advertise, and on which retailer, it's time to decide on targeting. Targeting on BookBub is simple: you just have to select a combination of (1) genre and (2) comp author(s).

For example, if I were advertising a spy thriller, the following targeting would be a good bet:

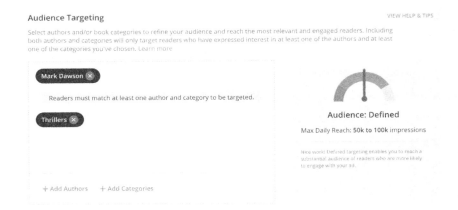

You might wonder why I chose an indie author like Mark Dawson rather than an uber-famous author like Lee Child or Michael Connelly. The reason is simply that the best author targets on BookBub tend to be famous or semifamous indie authors—definitely not big traditionally published authors.

To understand why, you need to understand what BookBub does with the author targets you put in there and how they use them to target readers. In short, if you put in "Author A," BookBub will show your ad to:

- All the "followers" of Author A on BookBub
- All the readers who have clicked on a Featured Deal title by this author in the past

So why will targets like "Lee Child" probably not work? Because there are tons of readers who follow these authors on BookBub because they're famous and not necessarily because they're fans of the genre. Similarly, if you see a discounted book by Lee Child in a BookBub newsletter, you might be tempted to click on it even if you don't usually read thrillers.

So the BookBub "readers" of these famous authors will be a mixed bunch. In comparison, BookBub "readers" of Mark Dawson will probably be a lot more focused: true spy thriller enthusiasts.

How many target authors should you select? Generally, it's best to test only one at a time, but only as long as your targeting needle is in the "green." If it's in the "red" (audience too small), you'll want to add another author.

Image

The ad image is something BookBub asks for earlier in the process, but I generally recommend leaving it blank and going back to it only after you've set up your links and targeting. The reason is that you'll probably want to customize your image *based* on your links and targeting.

For example, if you're targeting Bella Andre readers on Kobo, you might want to have some copy on your ad image appealing to these readers—e.g., "for fans of Bella Andre"— as well as a "Buy on Kobo" button.

If you're advertising an audiobook, you'll definitely want to have something on the image that clearly signals it, like headphones or speakers.

While BookBub has a built-in ad image creation tool, it will generate standard ad images with your cover, a dark background, some text, and a Buy button. Not bad, but you can definitely do better on your own with a tool like Canva or Book Brush. Both have a free plan, so you can give them each a spin, but I tend to recommend Book Brush because they specialize in book ads.

In any case, make sure you have the following elements on your ad image:

- Your cover, ideally within an e-reader image or on a 3-D print book image, or both
- Some *short* hook copy: either a tagline, a review excerpt, or "for fans of ..." language
- Whether the book is discounted or free, and the discounted price
- *Optional*: a call-to-action button

Below are some examples of ad images I created for clients of mine who didn't mind me sharing them publicly, so you can get a more precise idea of what I'm talking about. But BookBub's blog will also have a ton of examples of successful ads for you to take inspiration from!

Budget and bid

Finally, you'll have to set a budget for the campaign and decide on your bid. Since the purpose of your first BookBub ad campaigns will be to test audiences and images, you'll want to use a budget for each campaign big enough to produce statistically significant results, but not so big that all these tests will empty your bank account. I generally use either ten dollars or fifteen dollars, depending on the size of the audience.

As for the bid, you'll want to stick to the higher end of the range shown by BookBub in order for your campaigns to serve quickly and produce results. The quicker the ads gather impressions and clicks, the faster you'll know what works and what doesn't.

Finally, you see BookBub gives you the option to choose between CPC (cost per click) and CPM (cost per one thousand impressions). With CPC, you tell BookBub exactly how much you're ready to spend to generate a click. That's a great way to make sure you don't spend more than you want to per click, but if you set an unrealistic CPC target, BookBub simply won't serve your ad.

What's an unrealistic CPC target? Well, that entirely depends on how well optimized your campaign is. If you've nailed your targeting and ad image, you can get clicks for as cheap as $0.20 each on BookBub. But generally, when you're in the testing phase, your CPCs will be much higher than that. That's why I recommend using CPM bidding in the beginning—this will ensure that your campaigns get delivered and gather impressions and clicks. Once you've found a solid targeting and creative mix, you can switch to CPC bidding to control your spend. Not before opening a bottle of champagne to celebrate, though, because I can assure you that finding a *solid* targeting/creative mix is no easy feat. It takes testing, more testing, and then even more testing.

45

BookBub Ads II: Testing, testing, and more testing

Setting up an ad on BookBub is easy. Getting some clicks and initial traction is easy as well. But getting these ads to a point where they're profitable ... well, that's another story.

The good thing is, the road to the perfect BookBub ad is pretty straightforward. The bad thing is that it's long. Very long.

Your goal: Boosting the CTR

The *one* metric you should focus on with BookBub ads is the click-through rate (or CTR). Everything else will depend on it. The higher the CTR, the lower your cost per click and the cheaper it'll be for your ad to reach more people.

At the end of the day, what BookBub wants is to serve *relevant* ads to their readers, i.e., ads that they are interested in and click on. Ads that do not get clicks still make BookBub money (if you're using CPM bidding), but provide a bad experience for BookBub's end customer: the reader. So naturally, BookBub's algorithm will make it easier (read: cheaper) for high-CTR ads to reach more readers.

So how do you boost your CTR? There's only one way: finding the perfect targeting/image mix. And for that, you need to test both elements methodically, one at a time.

Step 1: Test your images

I generally like to start testing the creative, i.e., the image. I design one ad and four to five very different variations. By "very different," I mean images with a different background, different colors, a different disposition, etc.

Then I select *one* author target (or a mix) that seems to make the most sense, and set up four to five different ads targeting that same author (or mix), each with a different image. I spend ten to fifteen dollars on each and check in after a few days to see which had the best CTR: that's my "winning image" for this first round of testing.

Note: If you set several ten dollar ads targeting the same audience, you need to make sure the audience is big enough that the ads won't cause too much "fatigue." Any audience between ten thousand and fifty thousand will do the trick.

Step 2: Test your targets

Now that I have a "winning image," I'll use it to run some targeting tests, applying the same logic. I'll find four to five different author targets (with a big enough audience), and set up an equivalent number of ads, all with the same image and each targeting a different author. At the end of the test, I'll check to see which ad has the highest CTR, and that will be my "winning targeting/image mix."

Name	Status	Date Range ▾	Effective CPM	Effective CPC	Remaining Budget	Budget Spent	Impressions Served	Total Clicks	CTR	Actions
WB - 0.99 - Craig A. Falconer - Cover Background - Ebook	Completed	07/21/20 - 07/23/20	$7.59	$0.44	$3.79 (Total)	$6.21	818	14	1.71%	Select Action ▾
									Winning mix	
WB - 0.99 - Robert J. Crane - Cover Background - Ebook	Completed	07/21/20 - 07/23/20	$7.03	N/A	$4.03 (Total)	$5.97	849	0	N/A	Select Action ▾
WB - 0.99 - Bella Forrest - Cover Background - Ebook	Completed	07/21/20 - 07/23/20	$6.47	$2.00	$0.00 (Total)	$10.00	1,547	5	0.32%	Select Action ▾
WB - 0.99 - A.G. Riddle - Cover Background - Ebook	Completed	07/21/20 - 07/23/20	$6.98	$3.75	$0.02 (Total)	$15.01	2,151	4	0.19%	Select Action ▾
WB - 0.99 - Lindsay Buroker - Cover Background - Ebook	Completed	07/21/20 - 07/23/20	$7.36	$1.36	$0.00 (Total)	$15.01	2,038	11	0.54%	Select Action ▾

Same creative

"OK, but how do I find relevant author targets?"

Excellent question, especially considering that most author targets that tend to work well on Amazon ads *don't* work that well on BookBub. BookBub is a peculiar platform, and you'll probably need to do a lot of digging and testing until you find those "golden audiences." But to get started, just open your book's page on Amazon and scour through the Also Boughts. Note down all the names of the authors whose books look like a close fit to yours, and then head to BookBub's ad creation interface.

There, plug in the names to test whether they have an audience on BookBub. If BookBub says they have fewer than five thousand readers, then it's probably not worth targeting them—you can dismiss them. If they have more than five thousand readers, they're worth a try.

I recommend keeping track of all your author targets in a spread-sheet—even those you end up discarding because they don't have enough "readers" on BookBub. You'll probably have to repeat this operation several times when hunting for new audiences, so knowing whom you've tested before will be a big help.

Step 3: Retest images, then retest audiences, then ...

After the two tests above, you'll end up with a winning targeting/image mix. But that doesn't mean it's the perfect one—and it might not even be a good one. It's just the best one out of the ten or so tests you've run so far.

"*OK, but then* what *is considered a good targeting/image mix?*" According to BookBub ads expert David Gaughran, it's anything that yields you a 2 percent CTR or more. And I tend to second that advice. Two percent is definitely not an easy target to reach, but it's not impossible, and if you have an ad with a 2 percent CTR or higher, it's likely a profitable one.

I've personally never reached that target after two rounds of testing. So if after testing images and author targets, your best mix only gives you a 1 percent CTR, don't despair! Instead, go back to the testing board, design more image variants, hunt for more author targets, and keep testing both—always one at a time.

I know authors who've gotten to a 10 percent CTR or higher on BookBub ads, but only after *more than one hundred tests.* In other words: be patient, be methodical, and be persistent.

BookBub Ads resources

I mentioned I'm not an expert on running Amazon ads, and I have to confess that I'm even less of an expert on running BookBub ads—mostly because I lack the patience and persistence required to set up dozens and dozens of ads. After a while, I tend to give up and focus on Facebook ads instead.

That said, I'm good friends with someone who *definitely* is a BookBub ads expert: David Gaughran, who wrote a book with this very title: *BookBub Ads Expert.*[51] This is by far the number-one resource I recommend if you want to perfect your BookBub advertising game.

46

Facebook ads I: The structure

I still remember one of my first chats with Mark Dawson, back in 2015, at a happy hour organized by the Alliance of Independent Authors in London. Reedsy was barely getting started back then, and Mark recommended me to give Facebook ads a try to promote the business. "They're working really well for my books right now; it's quite incredible," he told me.

Fast-forward five years, and not only have Mark and I been using Facebook ads successfully for our respective businesses, he has trained thousands of authors through his courses, many of whom went on to make a living *thanks* to advertising their books on Facebook.

At this point, there is no doubt that Facebook advertising is one of the best channels authors can use to market their books. It is, however, a complex channel to master. There is a reason Mark put together *a whole course* around Facebook ads, and why so many books on them have been published: it's not easy to get started without some proper guidance.

I myself am working on a full book just on Facebook advertising, as it's the one marketing channel I use the most with my private author clients. And that book is probably going to be another fifty thousand words ... which I definitely cannot sum up in a few chapters here.

Instead, I'll do what I did for Amazon and BookBub in the previous chapters: give you the basics to *get started* on Facebook and set up your first ads, as well as some hints on how to monitor and optimize them. After that, it's up to you to further your education by taking a course or reading a book (*my* book, when it's out!).

Campaigns, ad sets, ads: Understanding the Facebook Ads pyramid

Before I venture into the ad creation process, it's important to understand how Facebook's advertising platform is structured—otherwise, you'll quickly get lost navigating it.

You can think of that structure like a pyramid, with "campaigns" at the top, "ad sets" in the middle, and "ads" at the bottom.

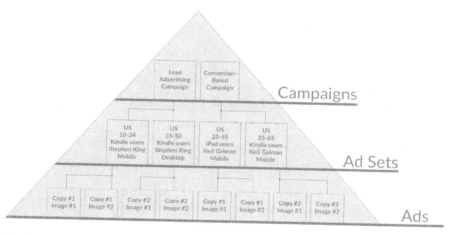

Let's go through the different levels and see what they contain.

Level 1: Campaign

The campaign level determines the type of ads you'll get to serve. Facebook makes it easy: you choose the campaign based on your objective.

- Get likes for your Facebook page: I almost never recommend this. Getting likes is as expensive on Facebook as getting leads, so why not get leads directly?

- Get clicks to your website: this is perfect for promoting content to a specific audience.
- Get video views: this is great for building awareness with a trailer before a launch.
- Generate conversions: your ads link to a page where users can sign up (or purchase). Facebook will optimize your ads for conversion.
- Collect leads: pretty powerful stuff. This lets Facebook users share info (like an e-mail address) without leaving Facebook.

As authors, you'll be using the "traffic" objective (get clicks) for the vast majority of your ads—unless you run ads to build your mailing list, in which case you'll want to try lead ads or conversion ads to BookFunnel.

At the campaign level, you can also opt in or out of "campaign budget optimization" (or CBO as we call it):

- With CBO, you set the budget at the campaign level, and Facebook autodistributes it across your ad sets to get you the cheapest cost per result.
- Without CBO, you set the budget at the ad set level, ensuring that *each* of your ad sets (and audiences) gets impressions and clicks.

If you're just starting out, I recommend not using CBO, as you'll want to *test* your audiences first. CBO is a good option, however, once you've found several audiences that work well and you want to group them in a campaign.

Level 2: Ad sets

Now that you've created your campaign, you can go into the ad set level to control:

- The audience you want to target
- The "placements," i.e., where you want your ad to appear (desktop news feed, desktop right column, mobile news feed, Instagram, etc.). Face-

book offers an autotargeting option for placements, which I *generally* recommend using.

- The daily budget you want to allocate to the particular audience and placements (if you haven't opted into CBO).

You can—and should—create several ad sets within one campaign to test different audiences and placements.

The ad set level is also where you can opt into *dynamic ads.* These are pretty powerful as they allow you to multitest several ad images and copy variations *within the same ad.* Dynamic ads also tend to offer a better cost per result than "normal" ads, so I encourage you to tick that box.

Level 3: The ads

At this level, you will design your ads by writing the copy and adding an image/video—or several copy and image/video options, in the case of dynamic ads. Facebook will offer you a preview of how your ad will look on the different placements you selected, which is particularly useful to determine how long your headline and text can be before they get cut off or hidden behind a "Read more."

In the case of nondynamic ads, you can create as many ads as you want in an ad set ... but that doesn't mean Facebook will show them all equally! It will run a test to determine which ad performs better and almost exclusively show that one going forward. If you want to run a test in which all your ads get an equal share of impressions, you should set up a specific "split test."

In the case of dynamic ads, you can only have one dynamic ad per ad set, containing all the variations you want for the copy elements and the image. Similarly, Facebook will run some tests with your different variations in the beginning and then concentrate your spend on the ones that perform best.

47

Facebook ads II: Creating your first ad

Now that you understand how the Facebook Ads platform is structured, it's time to dive in and set up your first ad! In this example, we'll set up an ad for a first-in-series, with the aim to drive traffic straight to the Amazon book page.

As such, we'll want to select a "traffic" objective for the campaign. And since we're just testing at this point, it's best to not opt into Campaign Budget Optimization (CBO).

Quick creation	Switch to Guided Creation ✕

Create New Campaign ▼

Campaign name	My first campaign|
Special ad category	☐ I'm creating a campaign for ads in a special ad category.
	Ads about credit, employment, housing, or social issues, elections or politics.
Buying type	Auction ▼
Campaign objective	⌖ Traffic ▼
⚗ A/B test ⓘ	◯
Campaign budget optimisation ⓘ	◯

Note: The Facebook ads platform will update and change design
more often than I will update this book. So don't be surprised
if your interface looks different¬--the elements themselves
probably won't be that different.

Creating your first audience

This is probably the most important bit of the process: deciding who is going to see your ads on Facebook—or in other word, your target audience.

All this is determined in the ad set section, and Facebook gives you a near-infinite set of targeting options to play with.

First, you can use some simple demographics to restrict your ads to certain genders or age groups, countries, or even regions. You can get incredibly granular with this, e.g., target 43-year-old females living in a particular neighborhood—but in 99 percent of cases you'll want to go relatively broad for a couple of reasons. First, if your target audience is too small, your costs will go up very quickly, because you'll be reaching the same people over and over again, and they'll stop clicking on or interacting with your ad. More importantly, books are consumer products that have huge audiences. It's not like you're selling a high-value product (e.g., a car) that only certain demographics can afford. And it's not like you're selling something *local.* Anyone in the US can buy a book.

So my recommendation is to avoid restricting yourself too much with the demographics. Of course, if you write romance, you might want to target only women over 30. Or if you write military science fiction, you might want to restrict your targeting to men. But for example, if you write young adult fantasy, I definitely wouldn't restrict your targeting to young adults, because YA is a category read by adults as much as (if not more than) teens.

Another reason for going broad with demographics is that Facebook gives you additional targeting tools that are a lot more interesting than just age, gender, or location. It gives you *Interests.* And that's something you'll want to spend some time researching, because it's probably the most important bit of a successful Facebook advertising campaign.

Finding relevant Facebook interests

What are "Facebook interests?" In the words of Facebook[52]:

```
Interests allows you to refine your ad's target audience based
on what they've included in their profiles, as well as the
Pages, groups and other things on Facebook they've connected
with.
```

Interests allows you to refine your ad's target audience based on what they've included in their profiles, as well as the Pages, groups and other things on Facebook they've connected with.

This is incredibly powerful because it lets you target Facebook users who are fans of, say, Stephen King, J. K. Rowling, or Ursula K. Le Guin. And Interests aren't limited to author names, but also include book titles: you can target fans of *Gone Girl*, *To Kill a Mockingbird*, or *The 4-Hour Workweek*, to give you a few well-known examples.

Of course, the more famous your target is, the less relevant the audience may be. For example, if you've written a young adult/middle-grade fantasy, "Harry Potter" will be an obvious option. But nowadays, the vast majority of Harry Potter fans are not heavy YA fantasy readers. Mainstream breakout best sellers draw an audience far broader than their genre, and are therefore not always your best bet. Instead, you might want to start with Interest targets that are a bit more niche.

Now, the big difference between Facebook ads and Amazon or BookBub ads is that you can't just target any author's fans on Facebook. Most authors won't have a dedicated Interest on Facebook; only the famous ones will. So your goal is to find those authors and book titles that are *famous enough to* have an Interest target on Facebook, but *not so famous* that they have a huge crossover appeal.

"OK, then how do I find such nonobvious Interests targets?" Well, the process is going to be a bit manual. For this research phase, I recommend that you go to "Facebook Audience Insights," which you can access through the menu navigation of the Facebook Ads interface (or by googling it). There, you'll be

276

able to not only test author names to see if they have an audience, but also view the demographics of said audience and find other similar authors to test.

I'll illustrate the process through an example. Let's say I've written a great epic fantasy and I'm looking for targets on Facebook. "The Lord of the Rings," "J. R. R. Tolkien," or "George R. R. Martin" are all obvious Interests, but may be a bit too broad. Instead, I'll want to test, say, "Brandon Sanderson" to see whether he has an Interest audience on Facebook. I'll enter it in the Interest box of the Facebook Audience Insights:

I see that he indeed has an audience of sixty thousand to seventy thousand people in the US. Even more interesting, I can now *analyze* his audience and find other similar targets. To do so, I'll head to the Page Likes section of Audience Insights:

The Top Categories section already gives me plenty more ideas to test: "The Stormlight Archive," "The Wheel of Time," "The Hobbit," "Robert Jordan," "Terry Goodkind," etc.

If I scroll down, I get even more ideas through the Page Likes section, which highlights the *affinity* between the Brandon Sanderson audience and several Facebook Pages. In other words, it shows us how likely our audience is to like a given Page compared to everyone on Facebook.

INTERESTS > ADDITIONAL INTERESTS	6 Arts & entertainment	Geek & Sundry
Brandon Sanderson	7 Book series	A Game of Thrones - A Song of Ice and Fire by George R R Martin
Connections	8 Community	Dungeons and Dragons Memes • Fantasy and Sci-Fi Rock My World
Pages	9 Games/Toys	Dungeons & Dragons • The Elder Scrolls • Diablo • Assassin's Creed
People Connected to	10 Publisher	Tor Books • Dark Horse Comics • Marvel

See All

Page Likes

Page	Relevance	Audience	Facebook	Affinity	
Ta'veren Tees	1	5.5K	13.2K	1294...	
Dragonmount	2	6K	15.5K	1209...	
The Stormlight Archive	3	5K	16.9K	9074x	
Wheel of Time	4	16K	64.5K	7708x	
Brandon Sanderson	5	5K	22.8K	6786x	
The Wheel of Time	6	21.4K	118.6K	5603x	
Robert Jordan	7	7K	64.7K	3352x	
Tor Books	8	5.8K	61.4K	2912x	

I'd make a list of these and enter them, one after the other, in the Interests box to see whether they have an audience. This way, you'll usually end up with a list of five to ten different Interest audiences to target.

One thing to note is that these Interests don't necessarily need to be author names or book titles. In the image above, for example, we see that "Tor Books" has a lot of affinity with the Brandon Sanderson audience and is available as an Interest target. It's a book imprint, not an author name or a book title, but it's just as relevant.

If you're in a genre where you struggle to find good book-related targets, you can try film or television ones, or even video games. For example, *Firefly* and *Serenity* are great audiences for all things space opera, and *The Elder Scrolls* can be good for dark fantasy, too.

Finally, don't forget to try something as simple as your genre. "Fantasy books," "Military science fiction," "Romantic thriller," or "Memoir" are all available as Interests to target on Facebook and to analyze via Audience Insights.

"But if we're shooting for highly relevant audiences, why target films or video games?" Because in all these cases, you'll want to narrow these audiences using specific book-buying Interests.

Narrowing by bookstore Interests

If you target "The Lord of the Rings" fans on Facebook, there's a high probability that your ad will reach people who have never read an e-book and don't even buy their hard copies on Amazon. So if your ad sends them to your book's Amazon page, they'll never buy.

That's why you want to narrow your targeting to users whom Facebook has identified as fans or consumers of a specific online retailer: the Kindle Store, Apple Books, Google Play, Kobo, the Nook store, etc. Luckily, all these retailers have corresponding Interests you can target on Facebook.

Similarly, if you're running a price promotion, you can use Interests like "BookBub" or "Ereader News Today" to narrow your audience to deal seekers. And if you're promoting a free book, you'll find a heap of "Free books" Interests to target.

```
Note: Facebook offers you the option to use "Detailed targeting
expansion." If you tick this box, Facebook will expand your
target audience to all people they think are similar enough.
It's not something I recommend while you're setting up your
first ads and testing audiences. But if you find one that works
particularly well and you want to scale it, it's a good option.
```

Selecting your placements

The last thing you'll have to decide for the ad set level is where you want your ads to show, or what Facebook calls the "placements."

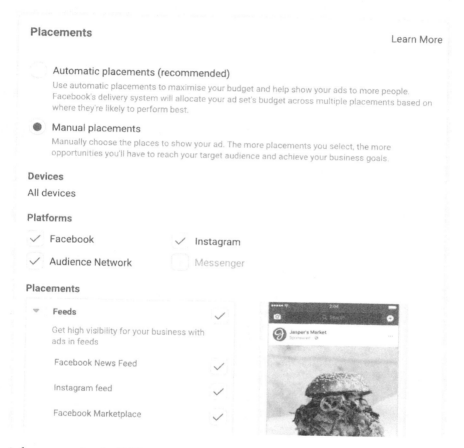

A few years back, I'd have recommended that you select "manual placements" and untick all the boxes that weren't "Facebook feed," and potentially "Instagram feed," as ads on other placements tended to perform a lot worse.

My recent experiences, though, have shown that automatic placements tend to outperform manual ones more often than not—especially in the case of dynamic ads.

Facebook will choose where to show your ad (placement) based on whom it's showing it to, and the type of creatives you've fed into the dynamic ad. (Don't worry, we'll cover that in the next chapter.) So selecting "automatic placements" gives Facebook more room to learn and auto-optimize, and tends to produce better results in the end.

That said, that's just my experience, and I know other authors who report a different one. You can easily test it by creating two identical ad sets, one with autoplacements and the other with manual placements restricted to the feeds.

Now that we've covered everything that goes into the ad set section, let's move to the ad itself and talk images and copy.

48

Facebook ads part III: The creative

So far, so good. You haven't had too much creative work, aside from finding Interest audiences to target. But now comes the part that will require a lot more work and inspiration from you: designing the ad.

A Facebook ad is composed of five essential elements. By order of importance:

1. **The image or video**, which you need to create yourself and upload to Facebook Ads Manager
2. **The headline**, which shows immediately below the image, in bold
3. **The primary text**, which shows above the image and can be a bit longer
4. **The call-to-action (CTA) button**, which you can choose from a number of presets like "Learn More," "Sign Up," "Download," or "Show Now." It shows on the bottom-right part of the ad.
5. **The description**, short text that goes below the headline, to the left of the CTA button

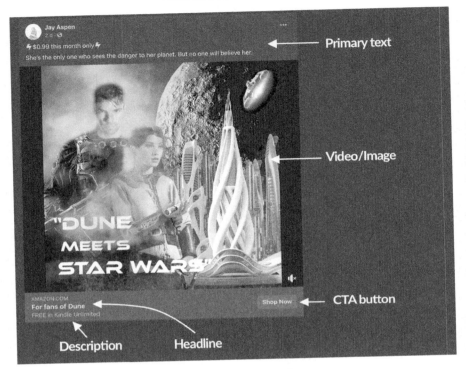

Facebook ad example

I'll go through each of these five elements in detail and offer some insider tips on how to create a winning ad on your first try.

Dynamic ads

Before I get to creative elements, though, I have to mention dynamic ads. These have been a game changer since Facebook released them, because they take a lot of work off your hands when it comes to testing images/videos and copy on the ad.

Here's the way dynamic ads work: you feed Facebook up to ten image or video options, and five options for each element of the copy. Facebook will then mix and match all these options to create dozens (or hundreds) of different ad variations, test them, and then zero in on the ones that perform best. Even better, Facebook then lets you see which image, copy, and CTA options have offered the best results.

To set up a dynamic ad, the first step is to make sure you've ticked the "dynamic ads" option on the *ad set* level. Then, when you go to the ad level, you can add several image and copy options:

"Normal" ad   Dynamic ad

To view the performance of your different image/video and copy options, you'll need to use the "Breakdown" drop-down menu, and select "By dynamic creative asset":

Now, I don't necessarily recommend removing all the asset options that are not the top-performing ones. The beauty of dynamic ads is that they offer *variety* for Facebook to use in different placements. Facebook might determine that a given image works well in the feed and another one works better on Stories—so removing one might hurt the ad's performance. Instead, I recommend that you periodically check your different assets' performance and eliminate the ones that clearly perform worse than the others.

In the example above, for instance, I'd remove the "Star Trek meets Dune" headline and potentially replace it with something else, but not remove the other two.

Now that you know why you should be using dynamic ads, let's go more in depth into each of the five elements that compose the ad.

The image/video

As you can see, 90 percent of the ad is composed of the image (or video), and that's by far your number-one tool to draw the eye of the Facebook user and make them stop scrolling and click to find out more. You have two options when it comes to creating your Facebook ad images: design those yourself, or have your cover designer do it. You did hire a cover designer, right? *RIGHT?*

If you're creating them yourself, then I recommend using Book Brush (but sourcing your own stock photo footage for the background). Unless, of course, you already have experience with tools such as Photoshop or Sketch.

Now, there has been some debate over the years on whether or not you should include the cover on the image. The reason is that Facebook used to limit the amount of text you can put on the ad image. The more text you placed on the image, the more it used to cost for your ad to reach people. (In technical terms, your CPM increased.) Your cover design naturally has text on it: your author name and book title, at least. So just having your book cover on the ad may have raised your cost per click.

While this rule is now gone, and Facebook officially doesn't penalize you for having text on the image, their data suggests that images with as little text as possible—or no text—do tend to produce better results.

All that said, not including the cover on the ad may lead to a lot of people clicking out of curiosity to find out what the ad is for, but not buying.

So all in all, after working with dozens of different authors in as many different genres, my conclusion is that it's something you have to test every time. To do so, you can set up a dynamic ad with several image options that *don't* feature your cover and run it for a few days. Next, copy it and replace all the no-cover images with images *featuring* the cover, run it for the same amount of days, and then compare your sales over the two periods.

Since images are worth a thousand words, I'm sharing some ad images that have worked well for several clients of mine, across different genres. This should be more than enough inspiration for you to create your first ad images!

The headline

The headline is probably the first bit of text Facebook users will look at if the image managed to grab their attention—or the second bit of text if you included text on your image, too. It needs to be something short and catchy, which will make readers want to click on the ad to find out more.

- Generally, I tend to use one of the following options as headline assets:
- The hook from the blurb: *"A deadly invasion is coming ..."*
- A review excerpt: *" 'I stayed up all night to finish this.'"*
- A reference to the Interest target: *"Miss Harry Potter? Meet [character]."*
- The price promotion: *"$0.99 this week only!"*

```
Pro tip: Try using relevant emojis in your headline! These are a
great way to catch the eye of Facebook scrollers.
```

It's important to note that if you use a longer headline, it'll eat up the "description" below on most mobile devices. This is not necessarily a bad thing, just something to be aware of so you include your most relevant message in the headline rather than in the description.

The primary text

The primary text shows up right above the image/video and makes the ad *look* just like a normal Facebook post. It's the one place where you can afford to put some longer copy (i.e., several paragraphs). Not that you necessarily *should*, but it's certainly something to test.

For example, you could have primary text that is a shorter version of the book's blurb, introducing your world and characters, and setting the stakes. In nonfiction, bullet points explaining what the book covers are also a good option.

Finally, there is also a case to be made for testing shorter primary text options that let the image do most of the talking and force the reader to click on the ad to find out more. I've had success with many different types and lengths of primary text, so again, it's something you'll have to test yourself.

The description

The description is the last element of text you'll have to come up with, and the least important one. As mentioned above, it will not even show on mobile devices if you have a long headline—and your call-to-action (CTA) button might also truncate it.

So you should keep your description text *extremely short* (think thirty characters or so). I often use it to list the price of the book, highlight that it's in Kindle Unlimited, or reinforce the call to action, e.g., *"Tap here to buy the book."*

The CTA button

This last element is much simpler: you just have to select a few CTA options from Facebook's drop-down menu. If you're promoting a paid book, I'd generally go for "Learn More" or "Shop Now." If you're advertising a free book, "Download" is a good option. And if you're running ads to a reader magnet to build your mailing list, "Sign Up" and "Subscribe" are worth adding to the mix as well.

Facebook Ads resources

As I mentioned, my next big project is to write a full book just on Facebook advertising, which will go more in depth into the different kinds of ads you can run, as well as how to scale performance, track conversions, and experiment with advanced creative types.

This book will probably not be ready before 2021, though, so in the meantime I'm happy to point you to two of my favorite Facebook advertising resources, which have provided me with both invaluable learning and inspiration:

- Mark Dawson's "Ads for Authors" course:[53] the most complete course you'll find on Facebook advertising (as well as Amazon, BookBub, and more) for authors. It's not cheap, and it only opens up for new registrations every semester, but it's worth every penny.
- *Help! My Facebook Ads Suck,*[54] by Mal and Jill Cooper: the first edition already was a must-read for any author looking to get started with Facebook ads, and this second edition has even more advanced tips. I might not 100 percent agree with all the recommendations in the book (e.g., not putting the cover on the ad image), but I certainly think they are all worth *testing.*

IX

One book, many products

The great thing with books is that they can be packaged and sold in many different formats. Once your book is ready, you can publish it as a print book, an e-book, and an audiobook. If you have a series, you can group the books in box sets or omnibuses. And if you can afford the translation, you can make your book available in dozens of different markets.

In this section, I'll explore all these wonderful marketing opportunities that don't even require you to write anything new!

49

Box sets

If you've never heard of the term, a box set (or boxed set) is basically a set of related books—often in the same series—packaged into a single item and sold on retailers.

The most common box sets you'll see are groupings of books one through three in a series, or books one through six, which is sometimes also called an "omnibus."

What's their purpose? Fundamentally, they give the author *another thing to sell.* And that is what makes them so useful, especially in today's book market that rewards fresh content so much. Have you ever heard that "the best marketing tool is to publish your next book?" Well, a box set allows you to do just that ... without having to write anything new! That's the magic of box sets.

"Yeah, but if people have already read the individual books, they're not going to buy the box set ..."

That's true, but here's the thing:

Box set readers are different

Anecdotal research (i.e., word of mouth in the indie author community) has shown that readers who buy box sets are, in general, different from your usual *one-book-at-a-time* readers. They're readers who shop predominantly for box sets.

So when you publish your first box set, you're not offering new content to your existing readership so much as you are presenting new content to a segment of readers you hadn't reached before. In other words, you're reaching new readers.

Speaking of which, box sets are one of the most useful strategies for growing an audience *outside* of Amazon. So if you're not exclusive to Amazon (or thinking about going wide), box sets should be a big part of your strategy.

Box sets and non-Amazon retailers

Since box sets normally aggregate several books, their price tends to be a lot higher than your regular $2.99 or $3.99 book. Most box sets of three books are priced above six dollars, for example. And for six-book omnibuses ... well, they can go well over $9.99, which you probably know is the upper price limit for getting 70 percent in royalties on Amazon.

Which brings us to the *other retailers*. Apple Books and Kobo both offer 70 percent in royalties on books priced over $9.99! And B&N offers 65 percent. This makes publishing high-priced box sets on these stores *a lot* more attractive than on Amazon.

This policy has helped these stores cultivate more of a "box set" audience. If you've ever listened to Draft2Digital or Kobo reps on conference panels, you'll know that they emphasize how well box sets perform wide *every time*.

```
Important: You cannot publish a box set wide if any of the books
in the box set is enrolled in KDP Select. Inversely, you cannot
enroll a box set in KDP Select if any of the books in it are
available on other retailers.
```

So here's a simple marketing idea: if you haven't published box sets and omnibuses already, do it! Even if you don't write in series, you can group some of your books together as long as they're relevant. And if you just have a standalone, you *could* partner with other authors to do a multiauthor box set and group your marketing resources and audiences to push it high up the rankings.

If you already have box sets out there, think, *What more could I be doing with them?* Here are some ideas:

- Put together a multibox set (how meta) at a high retail price, and make it exclusive to Apple or Kobo. (Their merchandising teams love exclusivity as much as they love box sets.)
- Assemble a box set of all your first-in-series books to act as an entry point into *all your series*.
- Make your digital box set available in print. You can format it super easily through our Reedsy Book Editor,[55] upload it to KDP Print and IngramSpark, and slap a thirty dollar price tag on it. Granted, it'll make a supersized doorstop of a book, but *some readers might buy it*. And it literally costs you nothing to make it.

Note that if you set up a paperback version of your box set, it cannot exceed a certain number of pages. (The exact number depends on ink, paper, and trim size.[56]) More importantly, you shouldn't name it "box set." Amazon doesn't allow paperback compilations to be called "box sets" as this could potentially confuse a customer, who'd expect to receive an actual cardboard sleeve with the individual books in it. Instead, you can use "collection," "omnibus," or other similar terms.

Of course, just putting a box set out there doesn't mean it'll instantly sell. First, you'll have to market it. So how do you market a box set?

Box set marketing: Try your usual suspects

When it comes to marketing these sets, there's no real need to think outside the box (ha!). A box set is ultimately a compilation of books, so the same tactics that work for marketing your regular books should work for your box set. Namely ...

- **Let your mailing list know about the box set release.** They might have read these books already, but if they haven't, they'll be more likely to buy the box set from you than purchase the individual books one by one. They trust you already, and a box set offers better value for money.
- **Run a price promotion.** If readers like getting books for $0.99, imagine how much they'll *love* getting *three books* for $0.99. Since discounting a box set from more than six dollars to $0.99 or $1.99 is such a high-value deal, price promotion sites and newsletters tend to *love* box sets. It's also no surprise that these often do particularly well on BookBub ads.
- **Advertise it.** Box sets give you two advantages when it comes to advertising. First, you can present them as a special deal, since they (should) offer the reader more value for money than buying the books individually. Second, they're generally higher priced than individual books. And higher prices mean better chances of achieving a positive ROI.

When discounted, box sets are ideal candidates for Facebook and BookBub ads. And at full price, they can yield you a steady stream of high-value sales if you promote them through Amazon ads.

50

Audiobook marketing

Most writers are fairly pessimistic when it comes to the future of the e-book market—a sentiment mostly fueled by Amazon's growing dominance. But if there's one thing almost everyone is excited about, it's audio. The global audiobooks market is expected to grow at a compound annual growth rate of 24.4 percent from 2020 to 2027,[57] and companies like Apple or Kobo have been investing a lot of resources into building their audiobook offering. They know they probably lost the battle against Amazon for e-books, and they don't want that to happen again with audio.

The problem with audiobooks is that they're expensive to produce. For a full novel, you can budget between $1,500 and $4,000 for the narration and production of the audiobook. This barrier to entry, however, means that the audiobook market is a lot less flooded than the e-book one—so it's a lot easier to get eyeballs on your audiobooks than on your e-books. Most of the authors I know who invested in audio made their money back (granted, not immediately), so I'd certainly encourage you to do the same.

All that said, simply releasing an audiobook doesn't mean it will start selling on its own. Just as with anything else out there, you'll need to market it a bit—which is what this chapter is all about.

Audio mentions and embeds

The first thing to do if you want to sell your audiobook is to make sure your *existing readers* know you have said audiobook. The more you *push* audio in your website and newsletter, the better your chances.

A great thing you can do is host samples of your audiobooks on SoundCloud, and then embed those on your website and share them in your newsletter. These clips can effectively act as a fun teaser.

Here's how to accomplish that with an Audible book:

1. Locate the Audible URL for your book.
2. Go to the handy Audible Sample Finder[58] website by narrator Steven Jay Cohen.
3. Paste in your Audible URL and click on the "Audio sample" it returns.
4. Click on the three dots icon and download that sample in MP3 format.
5. Head to SoundCloud, create an account, and upload your sample.
6. Click on "Share" below your SoundCloud soundtrack. Then click on "Embed" and copy the Embed code.
7. Embed that code in your website or newsletter.

Always send a newsletter when you release an audiobook. Some of your subscribers might have already read your book, but they probably have audiobook listener friends they can share the news with! Or they might *also* buy the audiobook to listen to it again.

Which brings us to ... Whispersync!

Whispersync, price promos, and the trickle-down effect

If you don't know about Whispersync, it's a cool Amazon technology that lets readers switch back and forth between reading the e-book on their Kindle and listening to the audiobook on Audible—without ever losing their place

More importantly (for us authors), it allows readers to buy the audiobook edition at a *deeply discounted* price if they've already purchased the e-book

Here's an example:

Now, this has created an interesting wave among freebie and deal seekers. Many audiobook listeners actively hunt for Whispersync deals.[59] And because they need to purchase the e-book first, they wait for the corresponding e-book to be discounted.

What does this look like from an author perspective? Well, if you run a reduced-price or free promo on an e-book that has an audiobook companion in Whispersync, and manage to get a BookBub Featured Deal (or replicate the effect of a Featured Deal through other promo sites), you'll see a trickle-down effect of *audiobook* sales after the promo.

Why? All those audio deal seekers will get your e-book for free or $0.99, and then buy the Whispersync audio for next to nothing! Instead of spending an Audible credit—or fifteen dollars plus—for the audiobook, they'll have gotten it for under five dollars.

Of course, you won't earn the same royalties on these Whispersync sales, since they're discounted, but in many authors' cases this trickle-down effect alone has actually *paid for* the BookBub Featured Deal.

Making the most of giveaway codes

If you use Audible's Audiobook Creation Exchange (ACX), you'll know that they offer authors up to fifty promo codes per audiobook and per country store (if you meet certain requirements[60]). These promo codes allow you to gift a copy of your audiobook to listeners, and can be used to distribute "Advanced Listener Copies" to get reviews on your audiobook.

One thing to note is that ACX promo codes used to earn authors *full royalties* when they were redeemed, and thus provide a rank boost on the store. As of March 2020, though, that is no longer the case, as the system was getting abused repeatedly by dodgy people.

If you don't use ACX and distribute wide via Findaway Voices instead, they offer giveaway codes as well. You can use these codes in the same way as ACX promo codes — except listeners will redeem those and listen to the audiobooks in Findaway's Authors Direct app, rather than on Audible.

There are several ways to do this:

1. You e-mail your list and offer them the giveaway codes (and ask that they commit to leaving an honest review).
2. You research audiobook bloggers and try to get them to review your book (which will yield you additional exposure to audiobook listeners).
3. You pay for a ten dollar Listen & Review ad in Audiobook Boom!,[61] which will quickly get you a bunch of requests from people in their list who are eager to review it.

Coreleasing e-book, paperback, and audiobook

This is an expensive strategy that requires both patience and money, but has worked wonders for everyone I know who tried it.

The idea is simple: release all your formats (e-book, print, and audio) on the same day on Amazon (and other retailers). Why is this beneficial, you may ask? Well, there are a few reasons.

First, Amazon is considered to favor books that have several formats available for purchase. Remember: Amazon's ultimate goal is to *sell products*. The more available formats a product page has, the higher the chance it will convert into sales. And nothing makes Amazon's algorithms happier than a well-converting product page. The same thing goes for all the other retailers.

Second, it gives your legacy readers the opportunity to try out your audiobooks. If you only release the audio version a month or two after the e-book, your fans will have already bought and read the e-book, so it's unlikely you'll make audio sales from them. If you release the audio on the same day as the e-book, they might go for the audiobook. Or—even better—they might go for both through Whispersync.

It's a pricey strategy, as you need to produce the audiobook *before* you make any money from e-book and print sales. But it's certainly worth testing if you want to step up your audio game.

Cheap first-in-series

One of the main struggles with audiobook marketing is that, if you're with Audible, you don't control the price of your audiobook. And as you know, price promotions are one of the easiest and most effective ways to market a book—whatever the format.

The good news is, other non-Audible distribution options are opening up, and *they let you control the price* on non-Audible stores. Findaway Voices is probably the most popular, and reaches all the major audiobook retailers and subscription services.

If you distribute with them, you lose the Audible-exclusivity benefits (higher royalties on Audible), but open up a whole new world of opportunity. You can run price promos (and try to get into BookBub's latest product, Chirp[62]). And you can also set up what I call "cheap first-in-series" on non-Audible stores.

Many series writers offer the first book in their series free or heavily discounted ($0.99), as a strategy to bait readers in. Well, that's a strategy you can now replicate on audio. And since audiobook listeners are so deal-starved (try to find good, cheap audiobooks on Kobo or iTunes ...), it's a strategy that will work a hundred times better than it does for e-books.

Audio box sets

And the final idea in this audiobook marketing chapter is ... box sets! I covered e-book and print box sets in the previous chapter, and the truth is, they work even better for audio.

See, Audible—the biggest audiobook retailer—offers a very popular subscription system where listeners pay a monthly fee and in exchange get *one or several* monthly credits to download an audiobook for free.

Now, say you're a listener with an Audible subscription, and you have one credit to spend. It will cost you the same to spend it on a two-hour-long audiobook as on a fifty-hour one. So which audiobook will you go for?

Size—or rather audiobook *length*—actually matters on Audible. And what's the great thing about audio box sets? You got it: they're loooooooong. So they offer listeners great value for money: spend one credit, and get three (or more) audiobooks. Even better, if you distribute your audiobooks through Audible, you have no control over price, but Audible automatically sets your audiobook's price based on its length—and pays you full royalties for any listener spending one of their credits on your audiobook. So the longer your audiobook, the higher Audible will price it, and the more money you'll make on each sale or "credit spend."

The last great thing about audio box sets is that they tend to sell *really* well when promoted through Facebook ads. "Audible.com" is available as an Interest to target, so just put together an image clearly signaling that you have an audio box set for sale (you can find some great templates for that on Book Brush), target a mix of Audible and comp authors, and give it a test! Make sure to use your Amazon affiliate codes or ACX bounty links[63] (if you have them) for tracking.

That's it for the audiobook marketing tips! I hope you'll make good use of them. Audiobooks are looking more and more like the future right now, so it's a market you'll want to get into sooner rather than later.

51

Translation: Entering new markets

If audiobooks allow you to reach new customers (listeners) in your existing markets, translations allow you to reach *whole new markets* and achieve the status of "internationally published author."

Before I venture into the nitty-gritty of literary translation and discuss whether it's something you should even consider, it's important to understand that there are different ways to get your book translated into other languages.

Traditionally, here's how books got translated: a local publisher would identify the book as having potential in their market, and would acquire the *foreign rights* of said book from the rights owner—usually, the publisher who initially published it in the first market. So for example, if a French publisher wanted to translate and publish an American book, they'd reach out to either the author's agent or its US publisher and negotiate to acquire the French rights to the manuscript. Once acquired, the publisher would have a literary agent translate it and would then release the translation to the French market. This is what we call "translation by foreign rights acquisition"—and until a few years ago, it was the only viable way to get your book into new markets.

In the early 2010s, though, several high-earning indie authors decided to take things into their own hands. Instead of trying to sell their foreign rights to local publishers, they went on to hire a literary translator directly and self-publish their books in those local markets. The advantage is that these "self-published translations" earn the authors a lot more royalties on each sale (70 percent, most of the time, for digital sales). The obvious disadvantage is that they can't get access to the traditional retail channels. And while that may not be a big deal in countries like the US or UK, where the vast majority of both e-book and print sales happen *online*, access to traditional channels is much more important in countries like France, Spain, or Italy, where physical bookstores are still the main retail channel.

That is, until COVID-19 happened.

The lockdown effect

In 2019, estimated e-book sales in France, Italy, and Spain made up for less than 6 percent of total book sales—compared to 30–40 percent in the US and UK.

Granted, these "official" percentages ignore the vast majority of self-published works (untracked by the ISBN system), so the real figures are probably much higher. Still, there's no denying the fact that e-books were just not that popular in Latin European countries.

There are a variety of reasons for that—which I won't get into here—but here's the interesting thing: the COVID lockdown of spring 2020 completely changed things up.

In France, Fnac (the second biggest e-book retailer after Amazon) reported a 130 percent growth of e-book downloads in March 2020. In Italy, e-book sales were up 50 percent just two weeks after the announcement of the lockdown. In Spain, e-book growth soared over 140 percent, and audiobook growth over 250 percent.

These numbers are crazy—and again, they don't even take Amazon sales into account, which is where most of the growth probably happened.

So what does this all mean? Well, it makes more sense than ever before to get your books translated and enter new markets.

How to get your books translated

The short answer is simple: you hire a professional literary translator. The long answer, is, well, longer. And it doesn't start with hiring a translator; it starts by researching the market.

1. Know the global market

Finding your niche and understanding your audience is one of the most important things when you're writing and selling a book in your own country, and *doubly* so when you're looking to sell a book abroad. Literary translators don't come cheap—budget at least $0.10 per word for a professional translation—so you should only get your book translated if you think you can *recoup the cost in sales.*

The key to coming out on the right side of this equation is understanding the global book market—and picking the ideal market to enter.

Broadly speaking, the most popular foreign markets for independent authors are Germany, France, Italy, and Spain.

The German market in particular is growing rapidly in terms of digital sales, so much so that Amazon decided to open up Amazon Advertising to Germany before any other foreign market besides the UK.

Lots of self-publishers also consider the proven Italian, French, and Spanish markets, especially for romance genres. While more "traditional" in their reading and book-buying habits than Germany (even after COVID), these markets are big enough that you can recoup your translation investment .. if you play your cards right.

"What about huge markets like China or India?" you may ask. Well, these are attractive because of their sheer size, but each presents unique challenges. China is known for its censorship when it comes to literary content. More importantly, Amazon doesn't exist there, meaning you'd rely on local online retailers for your sales—and if you can't read Chinese, you probably won't be able to understand how these retailers work.

India is known for its high levels of piracy when it comes to digital content.

More importantly, the country speaks dozens of different languages, so you'll never reach the whole Indian market with one translation.

All in all, I don't know any indie author who's done well by self-publishing a literary translation in China, India, or any Asian country for that matter. In contrast, I personally know *dozens* of indie authors who've recouped their investment on translations for the European markets. This doesn't mean you should rule out non-European markets entirely, but I'd definitely recommend that you only venture into those *after* successfully entering "easier" markets like the German one, and with a lot of careful research.

2. Research your target markets

Like any other big decision, you should choose your first foreign market based on a ton of independent research. Keep in mind your personal position, and don't make the mistake that a few unlucky protagonists in rom-coms make: just because something is popular doesn't necessarily mean that it's a good or right fit for you and your book!

Here are a few things to do before deciding to swipe right on an international market:

1. **Study the general state of the foreign market.** Besides making sure it's viable for your book, confirm its suitability for your specific genre. Fantasy might theoretically be a trendy genre in the Spanish market, but not so much in the Italian one.
2. **Check out the Amazon international marketplaces.** If you're interested in the German market, for example, review the books in your niche on Amazon.de. Do the same for the other foreign markets. This can help you gauge the popularity of your genre and your potential competition in that market.
3. **Review your existing international sales.** Have you noticed that some of your English-language book sales are starting to come from, say, France? Great! You've got a running start. It might be a good idea now to follow the (proverbial) scent and get your book translated first into

French—especially since you've already got that built-in French fan base, which will prove very useful when you're marketing the French edition of your book.

Though it might be tempting to cast your net wide, a good rule of thumb is to target only one market at a time. Just like big companies that expand internationally step by step, this will give you the opportunity to systematically test your book on new audiences. Until you've got at least two to three books out, it's hard to gain a foothold in *any* market.

3. Find a literary translator

Just in case it needs to be said: don't translate your book yourself. Don't even attempt it. Translating books into a whole new language is *hard*. You're not just translating words: you're translating ideas, and all of the subtle nuances that come package-and-parcel with English.

If you're serious about producing a quality translation of your book, there's no real replacement for a professional literary translator. Or rather a professional translator *with experience in your genre.* You might have a friend or relative who translated a few literature classics in the past, but hiring them to translate your military science fiction is *a bad idea.* Not only will they probably lack the niche vocabulary knowledge required for the genre, they won't be used to writing for your target audience, nor comfortable with your genre's palette of emotions.

Certain genres exert particular demands on style that won't faze experienced translators, while others require subject-area expertise. A romance translator, for example, is a master of swoon-worthy scenes, with an encyclopedic knowledge of all the local idioms for falling in love. A mystery specialist, meanwhile, has mastered the techniques for keeping readers on the edge of their seats, while a fantasy guru can come up with suitable equivalents for made-up words on the fly.

So how do you find a professional literary translator with experience in your genre? Well, I have no other choice than to shamelessly self-promote:

Reedsy. Not only have we curated some of the world's top literary translators for all the main European languages, you can search for them by genre and view all the books they've translated in the past. And if you can't find a good one for your book on Reedsy, drop me a line. I'll probably be able to recommend someone.

How to market your translations

Marketing a book is hard enough (you're reading a sixty-thousand-word book on the topic ...), so imagine marketing a book in a language you don't even speak. It sounds near impossible, except for two important things:

1. Foreign markets are *a lot less crowded* than the US or UK ones. There are few indie authors in Germany, France, Spain, or Italy, so you're competing almost exclusively against traditional publishers.
2. More importantly, if you've managed to sell well in the US and/or UK, it means your digital marketing skills are far superior to the ones of the average local publisher you'll be competing against.

Think about it this way: French, Spanish, Italian and German publishers don't care about Amazon categories, keywords, lists, and rankings. They don't run Kindle Countdown Deals. They rarely advertise on Facebook, not to mention Amazon. These are all things *you* know how to do—with a little help from your translator—if you've already successfully marketed your English editions.

And since you'll be one of the only few to do it, all these channels will be all the more effective, because the market is both less crowded and less competitive. Your price promotion will stand out more on Amazon, your ads will be cheaper, and you'll grab the number-one Amazon best seller tags easily in a bunch of niche categories.

With all this in mind, you should approach the launch of a foreign-language edition the same way you do an English-language one.

First, you'll want to nail your Amazon positioning, i.e., carefully research categories in the local country store. Note that the categories you see on the US store won't all be available on these smaller stores—so you'll have to browse each store independently, armed with Google Translate, to find all the relevant categories to list your book under. For keywords, you can simply ask your translator to translate your English ones. And the same goes for the blurb and editorial reviews: make sure to include those in your contract with the literary translator.

Once you've nailed your retailer presence, it's time to build your local street team. Remember when I mentioned that you should review your existing international sales before picking a new market to enter? If you have an existing, English-speaking fan base in a country, this will make the launch of the local-language edition a thousand times easier. Sure, these fans will have already read the book in English, so they probably won't buy the translation—but they probably have a ton of local friends who will! More importantly, they might be open to leaving a review on the translated edition, or—who knows—even offer to beta read it.

"But how do I contact these local readers?" Well, if you don't have a mailing list, you can't. But if you've implemented the advice in this book, you probably *do* have a mailing list. And most e-mail marketing providers let you *see* where your subscribers are (based on their IP address). So say you're looking to release a French translation: you could simply e-mail all your French-based subscribers to let them know about it and ask them whether they'd like to join your French street team.

Finally, I mentioned advertising briefly above, but it's worth expanding more on it, as this is where the biggest opportunity lies. There are a lot fewer people advertising books on Facebook and Amazon in Germany, Italy, France, or Spain. As a result, clicks are *a lot less expensive*, and ads tend to be all the more effective.

Mark Dawson is a great case study for this. In 2019, he started translating and publishing his books in Germany (enrolling them in Kindle Unlimited), and used a combination of Amazon and Facebook ads to promote them. In February 2020, he reported this in his Facebook group: "At the moment, I'm making around $750 a day in Germany, on a spend of around $100. And this is on a fraction of my backlist—there are another nine Miltons, two Beatrixes, and four Isabellas, plus standalones and collections."

The great thing with Amazon ads for foreign-language books is that you don't even need to know the local language. Most of the keywords you'll want to use as targets for your ads will be book titles and author names, and you can find those easily and copy/paste them from the Amazon Best Seller lists in your categories.

Facebook ads are a bit more complex, as they require you to create custom copy for them. But if your literary translator has already translated the blurb for you, you can ask them to come up with ad copy based on your English-language ads, too.

Because of the lack of competition, you'll be able to get clicks at an incredibly low cost in these countries. Some indie authors even use Amazon ads to promote their *English-language* books on the Amazon.de store—and turn a profit! So imagine promoting a *German-language* book that way: you'll achieve results similar to Mark Dawson's.

As your catalog grows, so do your opportunities to broaden and diversify your income streams. Box sets are an easy and inexpensive way to add more products to your catalog without any additional writing. Audiobooks take more time and money to produce, but make your words available to a whole new market. And finally, literary translations are even more expensive and time-consuming, but open the gates to the rest of the world. One single English-language book can, in time, turn into dozens of different products and income streams, which will contribute to building your brand and open even more gates and opportunities in the future.

Conclusion

Phew, you made it all the way through the book—or jumped straight to the conclusion in the hopes I'd reveal my best-kept secrets in it. If it's the former, congratulations. If you took the time and effort to sift through more than sixty thousand words about book marketing, it means that you're *serious* about your writing career, which is the single most important thing if you want to make it as a full-time writer.

If there's one thing you take away from this book, it should be that *you don't need to do all the things I discussed in it.* Seriously, you don't. Or rather you shouldn't. Otherwise, not only will you burn out at some point, but everything you'll do will be less effective, because you'll spread yourself too thin.

There are, however, many nonnegotiable elements, and I've covered those in Parts I through III of this book. You may have overlooked these sections because the advice in them seems so obvious and commonplace that our eyes tend to skim over it nowadays. And yet these are by far the most important because that's where 99 percent of authors fail. I receive e-mails every day from authors telling me that "marketing is the problem." Well, guess what? It almost never is. Let me illustrate why with a metaphor.

Imagine you're building a boat. If it's entirely made of lead, it'll sink no matter how strong the sails or the engine. If it's not well balanced, it'll kip. If it's not aerodynamic, it'll struggle to move. All these are nonnegotiable elements. Once you've got a boat that floats, is light, and is aerodynamic, then you can choose from any number of ways to push it forward: sails, thrusters, paddles.

Thrusters will push the boat faster—but they'll also be more costly Paddles are cheap, but require constant effort. And sails will move the boat on their own, but only if there's wind.

"Thank you for the obvious boat-construction advice, but can we get back to books now?"

Sure. Your book is the boat. If you write something that very few readers are interested in, your book will immediately sink. If it has the wrong cover, it'll kip under the pressure of polluted Also Boughts. If the blurb is bad, it'll struggle to sell.

But once you nail all these nonnegotiable elements, then *you can choose* how you want to push it.

Ads are thrusters: the more money you inject, the more they'll propel the book.

Daily posts on social media, reaching out to bloggers, going to reader fairs—these are paddles. They'll sell *some* copies, but at the cost of much manual effort, which is why they're not even mentioned in this book.

Retailer metadata and search engine optimization are the sails: they'll sell your book for you, but only if you climb high enough in the rankings or hit the right visibility spots.

So if you feel like you have a book—or a series—that just doesn't sell, no matter what you use to push it, don't blame the sails, thrusters, or paddles. Blame the book. Go back to the drawing board, fix all the nonnegotiable elements, and then try again. You'll be amazed at the results.

Notes

INTRODUCTION

1   Reedsy's weekly marketing newsletter: http://rdsy.me/newsletter

THE FUNDAMENTALS

2   50+ book marketing ideas: https://blog.reedsy.com/book-marketing-ideas/

THE CHANNELS

3   *Traction*, by Gabriel Weinberg and Justin Mares: http://rdsy.me/traction-book

4   Interview with Justin Mares, one of the authors of *Traction*: http://rdsy.me/Justin-Mares-Interview

FINDING YOUR NICHE

5   Kindlepreneur's Amazon rank-to-sales calculator: https://kindlepreneur.com/amazon-kdp-sales-rank-calculator

6   Publisher Rocket: http://rdsy.me/publisher-rocket (This is an affiliate link, but I use this product myself on a weekly basis.)

7   K-lytics reports: https://k-lytics.com/

ENTERING YOUR NICHE

8   Reedsy Bestseller podcast episode with Jami Albright: http://rdsy.me/JamiAlbrightPodcast

SERIES AND UNIVERSES

9   Michael Anderle on series, beats, and emotions: http://rdsy.me/beatsseries

READ THROUGH

10 Book Report, a useful tool to monitor your Amazon sales: https://www.getbookreport.com/

COVER DESIGN RULES

11 2020 Fiction Cover Design Trends: https://blog.reedsy.com/cover-design-trends-2020

12 Cover design A/B testing experiment: https://blog.reedsy.com/marketing-value-professional-book-cover/

BLURB-WRITING TIPS

13 In-depth article on how to write a blurb for your novel: https://blog.reedsy.com/write-blurb-novel/

14 Use this book description generator to add relevant HTML code (bold, italics, headers, etc.) to your Amazon, Barnes & Noble, and Kobo blurbs: https://kindlepreneur.com/amazon-book-description-generator/

JUST HOW IMPORTANT ARE REVIEWS?

15 An updated, searchable directory of the best book review blogs: https://blog.reedsy.com/book-review-blogs/

BUILDING YOUR STREET TEAM

16 The Street Team, Reedsy's Facebook group: https://www.facebook.com/groups/reedsystreetteam

AMAZON RANK & POPULARITY LISTS

17 David Gaughran's must-read book on Amazon marketing, Amazon Decoded: http://rdsy.me/amazon-decoded

AMAZON CATEGORIES

18 Publisher Rocket (affiliate link): http://rdsy.me/publisher-rocket

19 Blurb & Metadata experts on Reedsy: https://reedsy.com/marketing/blurb-metadata-optimization

20 BKLNK Categories finder: https://www.bklnk.com/categories5.php

AMAZON ALSO BOUGHTS

21 David Gaughran's article on Amazon Recommendations and Also Boughts: https://davidgaughran.com/also-boughts-amazon-recommendations-engine-algorithm/

AMAZON URL TIPS & TRICKS

22 Amazon squashes Trump trolls' attacks on Megyn Kelly's book: http://rdsy.me/amazon-trump-trolls-megyn-kelly

23 Tools to create universal book links:
    Books2Read (for all retailers): https://books2read.com/
    Booklinker (for Amazon only): https://www.booklinker.net/

24 Amazon Super URL spreadsheet: http://rdsy.me/amazon-super-url

KINDLE UNLIMITED VS. WIDE

25 "KDP Global Fund Payouts," by Written Word Media: https://www.writtenwordmedia.com/kdp-global-fund-payouts/

26 "The Visibility Gambit," by David Gaughran: https://davidgaughran.com/the-visibility-gambit/

SELLING ON NON-AMAZON RETAILERS

27 Joanna Penn on selling direct: https://www.thecreativepenn.com/2020/03/20/sell-direct-get-paid-now/

28 "Ebook Distribution: The Complete Guide for New Authors": https://blog.reedsy.com/ebook-distribution

KOBO

29 Kobo retailers across the world: http://rdsy.me/kobo-retailers

30 Free course on Kobo distribution hacks: https://blog.reedsy.com/learning/courses/distribution/kobo-hacks/

READER MAGNETS

31 *Reader Magnets*, by Nick Stephenson: http://rdsy.me/reader-magnets

32 Authors Direct audiobook giveaway: https://authors-direct.com/giveaway-codes/

33 Interview with M. L. Banner: http://rdsy.me/ml-banner

34 BookFunnel's website: https://bookfunnel.com/

WELCOME AUTOMATIONS

35 *Newsletter Ninja*, by Tammi Labrecque: http://rdsy.me/newsletter-ninja

36 Erica Ridley's newsletter: https://www.ericaridley.com/
Mark Dawson's newsletter: https://markjdawson.com/
David Gaughran's newsletter: https://davidgaughran.com/following-free-newsletter

LIST SEGMENTATION

37 Bonjoro: https://www.bonjoro.com/features

CLEANING YOUR LIST

38 While BookFunnel and Prolific Works group promotions are organized by the authors themselves, BookSweeps ones are curated and therefore known to provide a better quality of subscribers: https://www.booksweeps.com/

WHAT IS A PRICE PROMOTION?

39 Reedsy's directory of price promotion sites, classified in tiers: https://blog.reedsy.com/book-promotion-services/

HOW TO GET A BOOKBUB FEATURED DEAL

40 Minimum requirements to apply to a BookBub Featured Deal: https://www.bookbub.com/partners/requirements

41 BookBub's tips on optimizing your submission for a BookBub Featured Deal: http://rdsy.me/bookbub-submission-tips

42 Free BookBub submissions calendar: http://rdsy.me/bookbub-calendar

43   Craig Martelle on landing his first BookBub Featured Deal (note: you'll need to be a member of the Facebook group to view this): http://rdsy.me/craig-martelle-bookbub

AFFILIATES AND TRACKING CONVERSION

44   Amazon Associates: Amazon's affiliate program: https://affiliate-program.amazon.com/

AMAZON ADVERTISING I: SETTING UP YOUR FIRST CAMPAIGN

45   Amazon Advertising creative acceptance policies: http://rdsy.me/amazon-advertising-policies

AMAZON ADVERTISING II: FINDING MORE KEYWORDS

46   Publisher Rocket (affiliate link): http://rdsy.me/publisher-rocket

AMAZON ADVERTISING III: MONITORING AND OPTIMIZING

47   *Mastering Amazon Ads: An Author's Guide*, by Brian D. Meeks: https://books2read.com/u/mBG21p

48   *Amazon Ads Unleashed: Advanced Publishing and Marketing Strategies for Indie Authors*, by Robert J. Ryan: https://books2read.com/b/3GdpqL

49   "Going Deep with Amazon Advertising" course from Felicia Beasley: http://rdsy.me/felicia-beasley-course

50   "Ads for Authors" course from Mark Dawson (affiliate link): http://rdsy.me/ads-for-authors

BOOKBUB ADS II: TESTING, TESTING, AND MORE TESTING

51   *BookBub Ads Expert*, by David Gaughran: https://books2read.com/u/brWajk

FACEBOOK ADS II: CREATING YOUR FIRST AD

52   Facebook interests: http://rdsy.me/facebook-interests

FACEBOOK ADS PART III: THE CREATIVE

53   "Ads for Authors" course from Mark Dawson (affiliate link): http://rdsy.me/ads-for-authors

54   *Help! My Facebook Ads Suck*, by Mal and Jill Cooper: http://rdsy.me/facebook-ads-mal-cooper

BOX SETS

55   Reedsy Book Editor: https://reedsy.com/write-a-book

56   KDP Paperback Submission Guidelines: http://rdsy.me/kdp-print-guidelines

AUDIOBOOK MARKETING

57   Audiobooks market stats: http://rdsy.me/audiobook-market

58   Steven Jay Cohen's Audible Sample Finder: http://rdsy.me/audible-sample-finder

59 A trick to save big on audiobooks: http://rdsy.me/whispersync-for-listeners

60 ACX promo codes requirements: http://rdsy.me/acx-promo-codes

61 Audiobook Boom!: https://audiobookboom.com/authors

62 Chirp, by BookBub: https://www.chirpbooks.com/

63 ACX's bounty referral program: http://rdsy.me/acx-bounty

About the Author

Ricardo Fayet is one of the four founders of Reedsy, a marketplace connecting authors to the world's top publishing talent—from editors to cover designers, book marketers, or literary translators. He's the author of several Reedsy Learning courses on marketing and a regular presenter at several prestigious writers' conferences: NINC, RWA Australia, and The Self Publishing Show Live, among others.

He oversees the marketing for all Reedsy products—Marketplace, Book Editor, Learning, Discovery—and is a big SEO and Facebook advertising enthusiast.

In his spare time, he enjoys watching football (or "soccer" as y'all call it over there), and carrying tactical analyses to explain why his favorite team won.

If you have any questions about this book, you can reach out to him at ricardo@reedsy.com. He promises to answer you in (first) person.

You can connect with me on:
- https://reedsy.com/ricardo-fayet
- https://twitter.com/RicardoFayet
- https://www.facebook.com/groups/reedsystreetteam

Subscribe to my newsletter:

✉ http://rdsy.me/newsletter

Printed in Great Britain
by Amazon